LOST OMAHA

LOST OMAHA

JANET R. DALY BEDNAREK

THE History PRESS

Published by The History Press
Charleston, SC
www.historypress.com

First published 2018

Manufactured in the United States

ISBN 9781467119849

Library of Congress Control Number: 2017963242

CONTENTS

INTRODUCTION

"Creative destruction." This is a term coined by economist Joseph Schumpeter to describe the capitalist process in which the old is "incessantly" destroyed to make way for the new. Historian Max Page used the concept to inform his work *The Creative Destruction of Manhattan, 1900–1940*, which focuses on the making and remaking of Fifth Avenue. And it is an idea that comes to mind when thinking about Omaha, especially since World War II. As the economy in Omaha transformed from one based largely on agriculture, food processing and railroads to one driven by insurance companies, universities, medical centers ("eds and meds") and other service economy businesses and as automobile-enabled suburbanization changed where people lived and worked, the landscape of the old Omaha gave way to the new.[1] And in creating that new landscape, much was gained, but much was also lost.

Omaha, as was the case with most U.S. cities, began the postwar period with a downtown that functioned as its singular vital center. People went downtown to shop, to visit the doctor, to do their banking and to be entertained. Civic organizations held their meetings downtown. And people went downtown to work. Omaha's downtown skyline reflected these many activities—for example, the Medical Arts Building, the Hotel Fontenelle and the Omaha Athletic Club. A large warehouse and manufacturing district—later dubbed "Jobbers Canyon"—hugged the riverfront, as did a major lead refinery. Over time, however, the function of the downtown changed. Shops (particularly department stores), bank branches, movie theaters, jobs and professional offices moved to the suburbs, following residential populations. As these functions left the downtown, the buildings that housed them lost their clientele, indeed even their original reason for existing. Though many served as highly recognizable landmarks, eventually they gave way under the force of creative destruction.

Not everything that made Omaha the kind of city it was in 1945 existed in the downtown, however. To the south lay the sprawling Omaha Stockyards and the packing plants that employed thousands. To the west, many Omahans spent their leisure time at the Peony Park amusement park or the racetrack operated by the civic organization AK-SAR-BEN. Over time, however, these, too, felt the changes transforming how and where Omahans worked and played. Though perhaps the most visible of the creative destruction that transformed Omaha's landscape centered in the downtown, these outlying landmarks also gave way to the forces of change.

However, they were not the first structures to give way to change. Omaha, founded in 1854, transformed from frontier outpost to city rapidly, ranking among the one hundred largest urban areas in the United States as early as 1870.[2] Wood frame building gave way to brick and then to steel and concrete. By 1912, the city boasted of the tallest building between Chicago and the West Coast, the nineteen-story Woodman of the World Building. The settled area of the city spread north, west and south from the riverfront. Old replaced new with regularity as growth and progress remained deeply entrenched civic goals. Though occasionally some would make note of lost buildings and other landmarks, Omahans were not much for looking backward.

That changed, though, in the late twentieth century. From the 1950s through the 1970s, Omaha's downtown experienced a very significant wave of creative destruction. And, perhaps because for the first time some Omahans began to challenge demolition in the name of progress, the landmarks lost in that wave have received a good deal of attention. The old Post Office Building, in particular, became a rallying cry for those who favored historic preservation over demolition. Construction on the old Post Office Building began in 1892 but was not completed until 1906. A local history notes that initially the John Latenser–designed structure was "destined" to last one thousand years "and would be an attraction to match the fabled castles of Europe."[3] What is not often remembered is that as early as the 1930s, many civic leaders came to see it as an eyesore and unfit for a modern city.[4] Apparently, in some respects, it was not a particularly well-loved building until threatened. However, the controversies over what was built in its place—a bank headquarters and a hotel that required the closing of Sixteenth Street—certainly added to the arguments of those who lamented its demolition. And the demolition continued as the 1970s witnessed the clearance of a block-wide swath of buildings from Sixteenth Street to Eighth Street for the construction of the Central Park Mall (now renamed the Gene Leahy Mall in honor of the mayor who championed its construction). The demolition of the first Woodman of the World building—Omaha's first skyscraper—as well as old city hall and the Brandeis Theater also date from this period. Though Omaha never participated in the federal urban renewal program, it nonetheless managed to clear a good deal of its downtown.[5]

This work focuses on a subsequent wave of creative destruction between the 1980s and the early twenty-first century. During those years, Omaha's civic leaders worked to build on the changes they had spearheaded in the 1960s and 1970s and in many ways to complete the transformation to a new Omaha—one in which the downtown would serve not as *the* center but as an important image center for the city: an Omaha known for telecommunications, insurance and health services, not brawny railroad and packinghouse workers. The Hotel Fontenelle and the Omaha Athletic Club felt the brunt of the changes that came to the downtown in the 1960s. As downtown lost its centrality and as social habits changed, both closed their doors by the 1970s. They had, however, survived the wave of demolition in the 1960s and 1970s. They, along with the Medical Arts Building, which held on to tenants a bit longer, would not survive a subsequent wave beginning in the late 1980s. Outside the downtown, Peony Park, which began as a way station, well out of town, along the old Lincoln Highway, closed as suburban sprawl prevented its expansion and changing leisure patterns took Omahans farther afield for their amusement park experiences. The AK-SAR-BEN racetrack and coliseum, challenged by other gambling and entertainment venues, gave way to First Data Resources, the expansion of the University of Nebraska–Omaha and the creation of a new urbanist development. The stockyards—which had lost major customers with the closures of the city's meatpacking plants in the late 1960s and early 1970s—finally closed in 1999, ending a long chapter in Omaha's history. And another long history ended with the demolition and cleanup of the ASARCO lead refinery along the riverfront as Omaha's leaders became more attuned to environmental concerns.

It is tempting—especially in a work titled *Lost Omaha*—to wax nostalgic about those urban landmarks that have disappeared since World War II. It is not difficult to mourn once vibrant and well-loved venues that are no more.

At the same time, while it can be appropriate to hold on to memories of those places, we must also recognize that cities can, do and should change—and whether those changes are for the good or bad is often a matter of perspective. This is not to argue for the comprehensive sweeping away of the past—the mind-set behind modernist architecture and much of the urban renewal program of the 1950s and 1960s—but memory can be a complicated thing. For example, while many may remember Peony Park for its dance bands and concerts, others will remember that its owners fought to keep its swimming pool segregated. The stockyards and packing plants provided thousands of jobs, but those jobs were often dirty and dangerous. And the yards and plants produced a tremendous amount of pollution. So did the ASARCO refinery, so much so that it resulted in the designation of much of eastern Omaha as a Superfund site. Omaha has held on to many buildings that help tell the story of its past, and it has lost others. But even when the buildings are gone, the story can still be told. Creative destruction may indeed result in demolition and replacement, but nothing is ever truly lost until it is forgotten.

CHAPTER 1

WHEN DOWNTOWN WAS THE CENTER AND WE DIDN'T "BOWL ALONE"

THE MEDICAL ARTS BUILDING

All three buildings highlighted in this chapter faced trials at one time or another during their histories. None, however, had as challenging a start as the Medical Arts Building. The troubles the "medical men" of Omaha would face in realizing their dreams of a major downtown office building were not evident when they first optimistically announced the start of construction in late November 1919 and the local newspaper heralded the start of the second-largest office building in the city. As planned, the new $2 million Medical Arts Building, designed by local architect Thomas Kimball, would soar to sixteen stories. Kimball, the son of a vice president of the Union Pacific Railroad, had served as the chief architect for the Trans-Mississippi and International Exposition held in Omaha in the late nineteenth century. Most floors would house offices for doctors and dentists. The first floor would include a pharmacy and surgical supply company; the fourth floor, Riggs Optical Company; the fifth, a dental supply company; and the fourteenth, a two-hundred-seat auditorium and reading room. A spokesperson for the Medical Arts Society of Omaha declared the concentration of medical services in the building would make it as "important as a department store" to the city, as it would bring the same level of convenience and efficiency. The society anticipated completion of the structure in February 1921.[6]

Financing, however, proved difficult in the wake of the recession following World War I. Construction finally began in late 1921, and by August 1922, a good deal of the structural steel work was complete.[7] Financial issues, however, soon halted progress. Although the local newspaper carried several stories announcing new arrangements, money troubles continued. In December 1923, architect Thomas Kimball asked the district court to force a sale of the unfinished building in order to satisfy his claim for payment for his services. The following year, creditors attempted to sell the unfinished building to the American Legion, and by August 1924, the local newspaper wondered if the building would ever be completed. In the meantime, plans for the building had been altered. Instead of a building constructed in a U shape with two wings off the main building, the new plans called for an L-shaped building.[8] Finally, in July 1925, Philip Gold, a Chicago attorney, purchased the unfinished building at a sheriff's sale for $200,000. He predicted that it would require $1.4 to $1.6 million to complete construction.[9]

The Medical Arts Building finally opened on September 15, 1926, when it hosted the annual convention of the Medical Society of the Missouri Valley. A directory of tenants, published in December 1926, listed over sixty doctors and dentists with offices already in the facility and twenty more who would soon occupy office space there.[10] That the building attracted the top doctors in Omaha was evident in the November 1929 article reporting the death of Dr. Harold Gifford. He and his son, Dr. Stanford Gifford, occupied office number 1620. Dr. Harold Gifford was an internationally known eye surgeon. Educated at the University of Michigan, Gifford also received extensive training abroad in Heidelberg, Zurich and Vienna. He came to Omaha in 1886. His patients came from all over the world, and he published his research work in a variety of prestigious journals. He soon became not just a prominent physician but also a vigorous civic leader. He invested in local real estate and later donated land for parks and playgrounds. He also donated land at the north and south ends of the city's River Drive—land he had purchased "to preserve its wild beauty from commercial development as real estate." Gifford headed the Department of Ophthalmology at the University of Nebraska for twenty-five years, retiring in 1924 as professor emeritus. In 1928, the Omaha Post of the American Legion named him the city's "most valuable citizen." According to the newspaper, Gifford was known locally as "an independent thinker" and someone who "spoke with vigor his beliefs as a socialist in politics and an agnostic in religion."[11]

Despite attracting the top medical talent in the city, financial woes continued. An April 1926 article in the newspaper declared the Medical Arts Building "the most heavily mortgaged building in Omaha and probably in Nebraska." In August 1930, the building went into

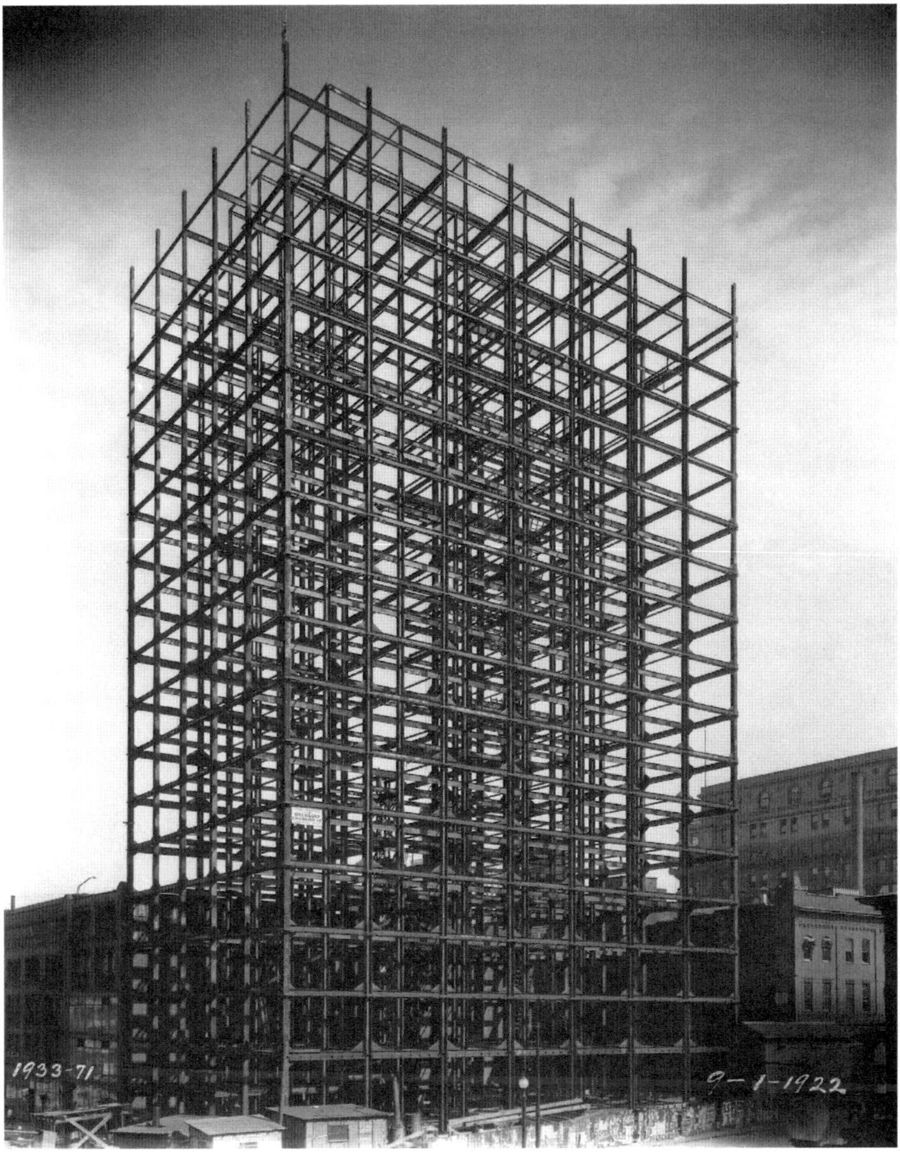

The Medical Arts Building under construction, a process that took much longer than anticipated. *Courtesy of the Durham Museum Photo Archives.*

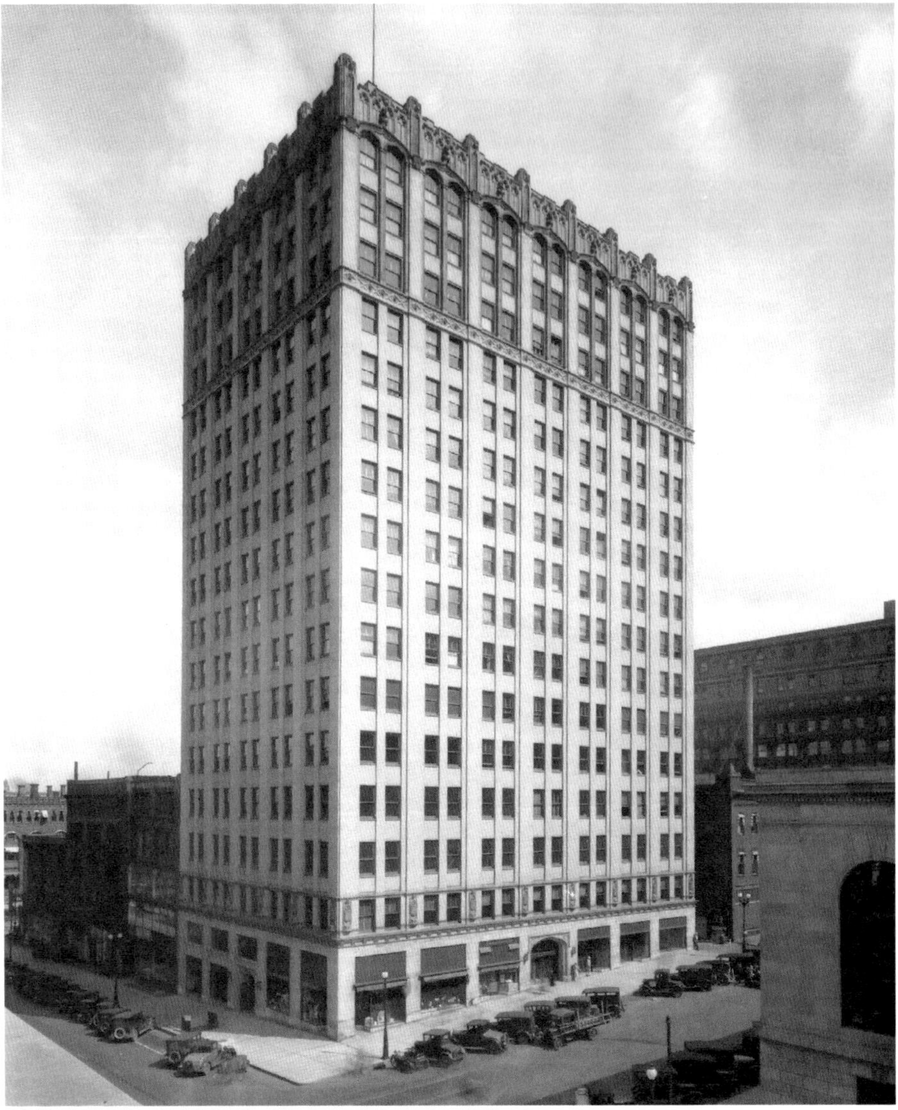

Medical Arts Building completed. Though the top doctors in Omaha had offices in the building, it never became a financial success. *Courtesy of the Durham Museum Photo Archives.*

receivership. Although the building was reported "85 percent rented," the Chicago group that controlled the building, headed by Gold, had defaulted on the interest payment on the bonds.[12] Once again, the building was sold at auction, this time to a group of its bondholders for $850,000. The United States Bank, named as the receiver in 1930, remained the building's trustee until the Connecticut General Life Insurance Company purchased it in 1947 for $1.2 million. The building continued to change hands. A group of Omaha investors bought it in 1961 and then sold it to Fidelity Corporation of Richmond, Virginia, in 1968 for $1 million. Fidelity then turned over the top seven floors as offices for its subsidiary, Central National Insurance.[13]

Central National did extensive renovation on the building. The top four floors served as the company's main office. Improvements included oak paneling, a "classic curved oak staircase" and "brass and crystal chandeliers." The penthouse served as the company's board room.[14] The company also renovated the building's auditorium. When Central National moved into the building in 1970, the two-story auditorium had not been used since the 1930s except as storage space. In 1980, the company restored the auditorium with its stage and motion picture booth as a venue for meetings and clinics. The company also planned to make the space available for community organizations and nonprofit groups. A spokesman hoped that making the space available for such meetings would contribute to the revitalization of the downtown.[15]

Money issues were not the only woes to befall the building. The Medical Arts Building had the first automatic elevators in the city. Apparently, though, many did not trust the new technology, and the building's elevators still employed operators. In March 1930, those operators—all women—reported hearing a ghostly sound in elevator shaft number three. They said the sound resembled that of a cat in distress. The "creepy" sound led the operators to try to avoid using that elevator at night, and reportedly one of the operators refused to work on Friday the thirteenth. The more practical-minded blamed the noise on the elevator's pneumatic doors. Others opined the noise was produced by the spirit of some cat subjected to a prank during the medical school days of one or more of the tenants.[16] And if a haunting was not enough, the building was also the site of at least two suicides—the first in August 1937 and the second, just over a year later, in October 1938.[17]

Despite these many difficulties, the building did serve as a center for Omaha's medical profession for most of its existence. It also played an interesting role in a not-too-well-known underground passageway in downtown Omaha. In 1971, planning director Alden Aust told a local reporter that a person could travel underground from the new Hilton Hotel (built on the site of the old post office) to the Woodman Tower (built on the site of the old city hall). Along the way, the route traveled through the lower levels of the Medical Arts Building, JC Penney's, Woolworth's and the Brandeis department store. The reporter decided to test the assertion of the planning director. He found that the part of the route from the Hilton through the new First National Bank building was blocked by construction. He was able to travel—though frequently having to ask directions—through the Medical Arts Building, JC Penney's, Woolworth's and Brandeis to the Woodman Tower. (The author remembers her mother showing her the route underground from the lower level of Brandeis to the Medical Arts Building in the 1970s.) The walk, though, took forty minutes. The reporter estimated that one could travel from the Hilton to the Woodman Tower on surface sidewalks in ten minutes.[18]

The Medical Arts Building was also well known for its cafeteria and specialty stores. In 1950, Faye Hosman, who also operated a lunch counter in the basement of the JC Penney Building, announced plans to construct a 206-seat cafeteria in the basement of the Medical Arts Building. The cafeteria was connected to the main floor of the JC Penney Building through an eleven-foot opening cut through the basement of the Medical Arts Building. (This was a key part of the underground route described above.) Although located in former storage space in the Medical Arts Building, the new cafeteria was named the JC Penney Cafeteria.[19] The Medical Arts Building also housed a special shop for the blind, opened in early 1961 in the lobby area. The Nebraska Foundation for the Visually Handicapped operated the shop and sold its products at cost.[20]

Though doctors and dentists continued to occupy much of the office space, in the early 1980s, the owners changed the building's name from the Medical Arts Building to Professional Tower, reflecting the presence of the insurance company and other businesses. However, many continued to refer to the building by its old name.

The Medical Arts Building, unlike the Omaha Athletic Club and the Fontenelle Hotel, did not shut its doors primarily due to a decline in business. Instead, the Medical Arts Building gave way to a massive downtown revitalization project. In October 1996, city leaders unveiled an extensive downtown redevelopment plan. It included new

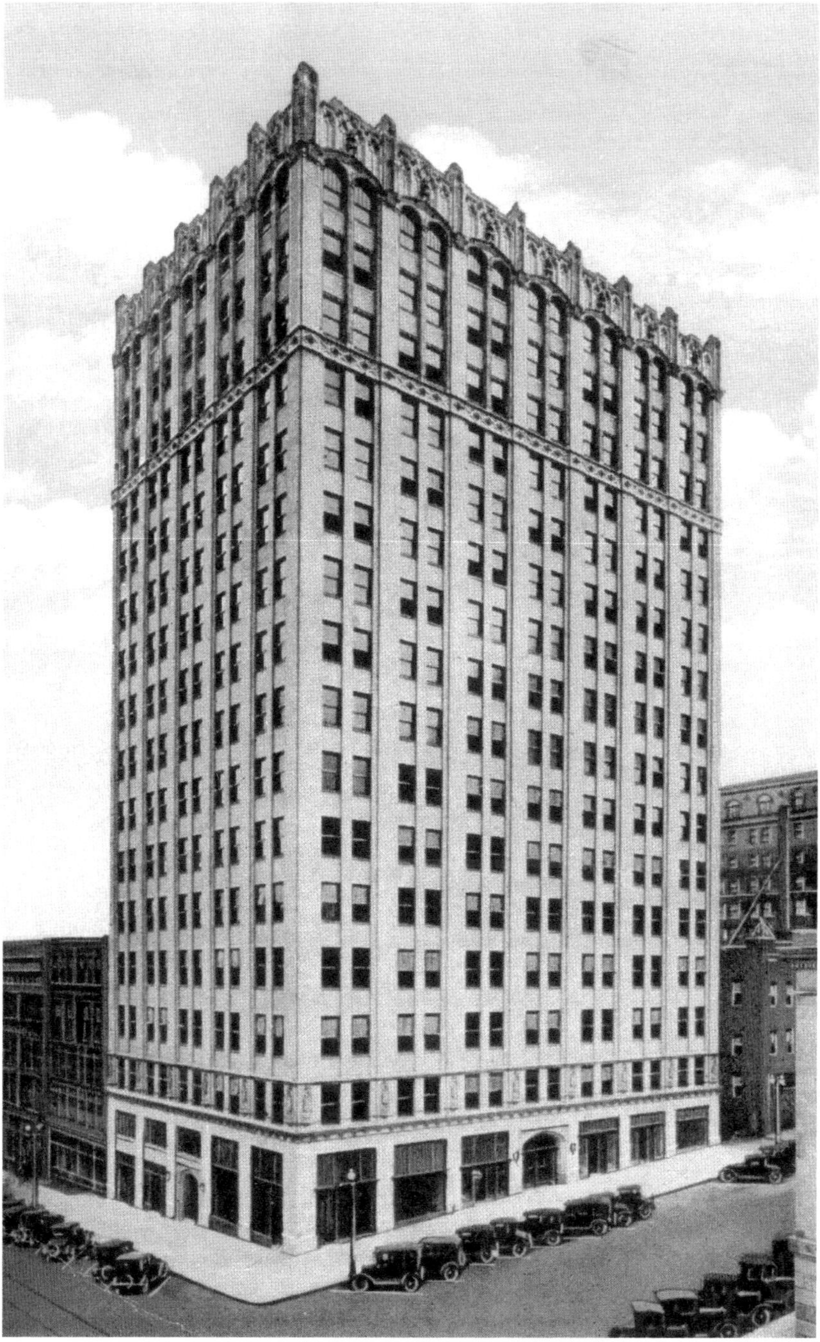

The Medical Arts Building was one of the many local landmarks appearing on postcards. *Courtesy of the Omaha Public Library Collection.*

building projects for the Union Pacific Corporation, the World-Herald Corporation and First National Bank. To support the project, the city created a thirty-two-block redevelopment area stretching from Douglas Street to Interstate 480, Eighth Street to Seventeenth Street. The creation of this area allowed the city to use tax-increment financing, revenue bonds and eminent domain to support the building projects.[21] The Medical Arts Building occupied the site slated for the new forty-story headquarters building for First National Bank.

Within a month, businesses located in the redevelopment area received notice, including tenants in the Medical Arts Building. Negotiations to purchase the building took time, but in March 1998, First National Bank purchased the building from Central Northern for $4.4 million. The last of the tenants moved out during the summer of 1998. Among those tenants was Dr. J. MacRae Williams, a dentist. He first opened an office in the building in 1957 and still operated his practice from Office 411 as late as July 1998. He was one of the last six dentists in the building and lamented the imminent destruction of the place where he had worked for "more than half my life," saying, "I would have retired in that building." Another longtime tenant, Dr. James Theisen, worked out of the building for thirty-six years before being forced to move. He compared the tenants to "neighbors in a community." He stated, "We all became friends in the building....I could always look out the window of my second-floor office and see someone I knew walking by."[22]

On April 2, 1999, Controlled Demolition of Baltimore detonated 175 pounds of explosives strategically placed throughout the building. Though a spring storm temporarily delayed the blast, shortly after 9:07 p.m., the seventy-three-year-old Medical Arts Building was a pile of rubble.[23] But not all the building ended up on the rubble pile. Bruce Lauritzen, chairman of the holding company that owns First National Bank, directed that pieces of the terra-cotta façade be saved. They now serve as a centerpiece of the bank's Winter Garden, located on the north side of the new bank tower. And it should be remembered that the decision to create the redevelopment area and clear the site did influence Lauritzen's decision to build the bank's new headquarters in downtown rather than suburban Omaha.[24]

Hotel Fontenelle

In 1913, Gurdon W. Wattles, a prominent local businessman and banker, organized the Douglas Hotel Company. He then set about raising money for the construction of a major hotel in downtown Omaha. Wattles had a good deal of experience organizing major civic projects and enterprises. He came to Omaha in 1892 as the vice president of the Union Bank. Three years later, he joined the board of the Trans-Mississippi Exposition Company and in 1898 served as its president. He was generally credited with the success of the Trans-Mississippi and International Exposition—Omaha's own "world's fair"—held between June and November 1898. He went on to serve as president of the Knights of AK-SAR-BEN from 1905 to 1907, and the organization chose him as its "king" in 1908. He also founded the Omaha Grain Exchange.[25] On Thursday, February 25, 1915, the local stockholders and their wives celebrated the grand opening of the Hotel Fontenelle.

The new hotel was named in honor of Logan Fontenelle. Fontenelle was born in 1825 in what later became Nebraska Territory. His father was a French Creole fur trader from New Orleans and his mother the daughter of a chief of the Omaha tribe. He eventually served as a leader among the Omaha people, traveling as an interpreter with a group of tribal chiefs who traveled to Washington, D.C., in 1854 to negotiate a treaty. John L. Webster, a local attorney and early president of the Nebraska Historical Society, presented a story of Logan Fontenelle to those gathered for the grand opening. Webster essentially credited Fontenelle with making possible the creation of the state of Nebraska and the founding of Omaha. The treaty that Fontenelle helped negotiate ceded the Omaha tribe's land to the federal government. Webster compared the treaty to the Declaration of Independence and the agreement that resulted in the Louisiana Purchase. The Treaty of 1854, he declared, opened the lands that would become Nebraska Territory the following year to white settlement. It also promised that the federal government would protect the Omaha people from the Sioux—a promise that was broken in 1855 when a band of Sioux killed Logan Fontenelle while he was hunting in what became Boone County, Nebraska. Webster heralded Fontenelle as a "martyr" to his people, adding, curiously, "The independent nationality of the Indian tribe perished [with the Treaty of 1854], but Pheonix-like [*sic*], the red man rose up to citizenship in the white man's government. Our nation has become their nation and our flag has become their flag."[26] Webster made his remarks in 1915, but Native Americans generally were not granted U.S. citizenship until 1924.

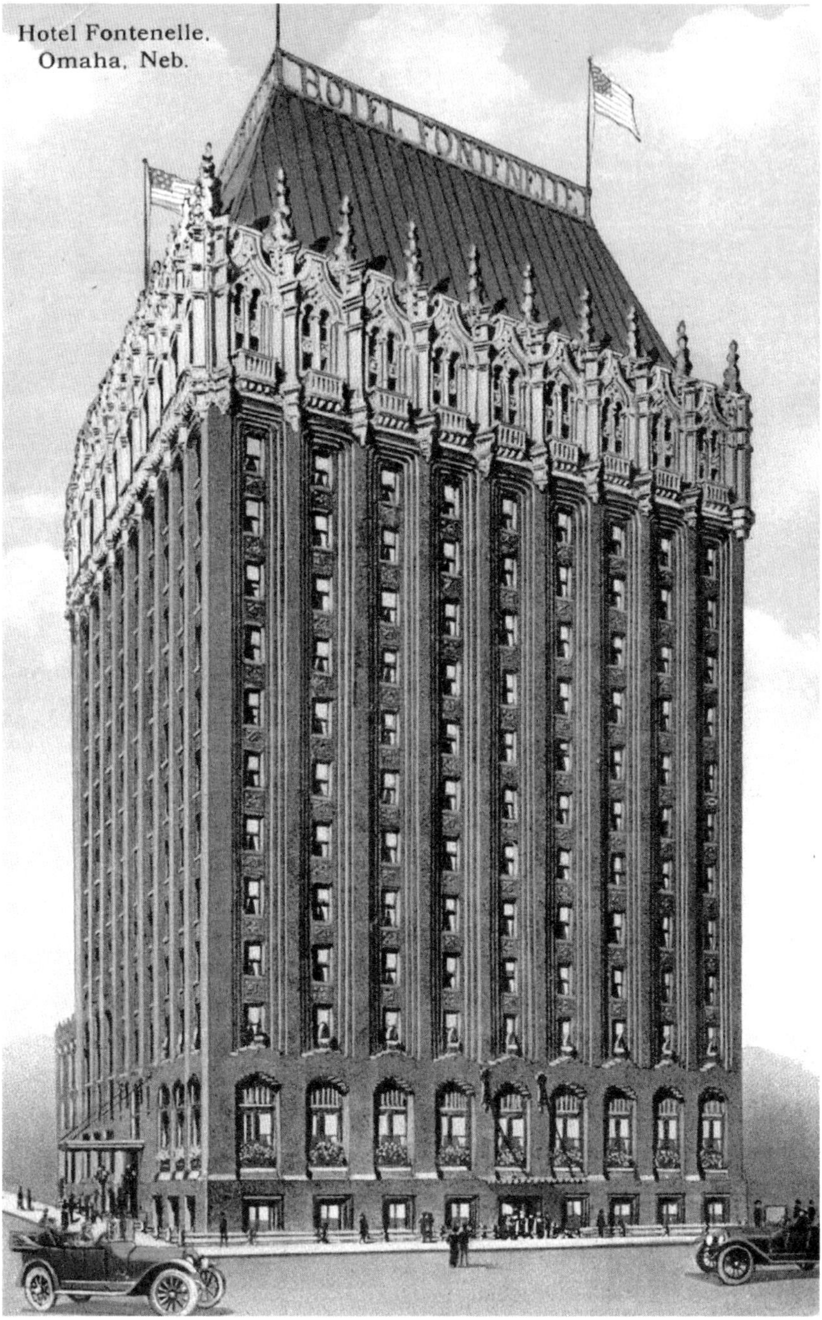

The Hotel Fontenelle was another downtown landmark that appeared on postcards. *Courtesy of the Omaha Public Library Collection.*

Noted Omaha architect Thomas R. Kimball served as architect for the new hotel. The design was described as late Gothic Revival. It had sixteen stories above ground, a basement and a subbasement. With more than three hundred rooms, the building quickly emerged as a local landmark. The top three floors of the hotel were faced with terra cotta designed to resemble the headdress of Logan Fontenelle. It boasted a five-hundred-seat ballroom, electric elevators and telephones in each suite.[27]

Just as with the Medical Arts Building and the Omaha Athletic Club, the Hotel Fontenelle got off to a rocky start. In early April 1915, just a few months after the grand opening, the hotel's manager, William Burbank, died suddenly of a heart attack.[28] And although the hotel did well during the war years, even hosting a major event to celebrate General John "Black Jack" Pershing's birthday in September 1918, the postwar recession and passage of the Eighteenth Amendment hit the hotel business hard throughout the United States.[29] For several years, many of the headlines featuring the hotel spoke of bankruptcies and buyouts rather than social events and conventions. That part of the story ended, though, with one of the most significant developments in the history of the hotel: its purchase by Eugene C. Eppley.

Eugene C. "Gene" Eppley was born on April 8, 1884, in Akron, Ohio. His career in the hotel business began at age nineteen when he purchased the McKinley Hotel in Canton, Ohio. In 1917, he formed the Eppley Hotel Company as an umbrella corporation to hold his growing list of hotel properties throughout the Midwest. After serving with the Fuel Administration during World War I, Eppley resumed his hotel purchases. In 1920, he turned his attention to the Hotel Fontenelle, then under the management of the Nebraska Hotel Company, which owned several hotels in the state. The Nebraska Hotel Company was in bankruptcy. Eppley agreed to pay $200,000 cash and then make monthly payments on the balance of the $1 million total purchase price. He took possession on January 1, 1921, and moved the headquarters of his growing hotel empire—and his personal residence—to the Hotel Fontenelle. Stockholders of the Nebraska Hotel Company challenged that initial sale, however, and in 1923, the Nebraska Supreme Court reversed the transaction. Eppley then agreed to pay $950,000 cash—though receiving credit for the payments he had already made. As no one challenged the sale, Eppley closed the deal on December 22, 1923. With the purchase finally secured, Eppley was one of the largest individual hotel operators in the United States.[30]

Eppley and the Hotel Fontenelle witnessed economic ups and downs throughout the 1920s and 1930s. Eppley, though, quickly established himself as a key civic leader. He helped found the Greater Omaha Association, served as a director of the Omaha Chamber of Commerce and was also the city's delegate to a River and Harbors Conference in Washington, D.C. His position at the top levels of the local business community was confirmed in 1933 when he was selected as king of AK-SAR-BEN. As part of the ceremonies, he hosted an elaborate celebration in the ballroom of the hotel.[31] For many years thereafter, he hosted parties in connection with the annual coronation ceremony.

Eppley and the Hotel Fontenelle played host to many important guests over the years. One of the first prominent celebrities to stay at the hotel after Eppley purchased it was the author Sinclair Lewis, in town to give a lecture at the hotel in April 1921. The author's visit was front-page news. The article stated that he had to borrow the reporter's suit for his photograph session and that he had four "flasks" in his hotel room—though the reporter noted that by the time of the interview all four were empty, much to Sinclair's disappointment. More than a decade later, Sinclair Lewis published *Work of Art*, a novel about a great hotel man he called Myron Weagle. At one point in the book, that character names those he considers the greatest hotel men in America and ends the list with Eugene Eppley.[32]

In 1939, Omaha hosted the premiere of the movie *Union Pacific*, starring Barbara Stanwyck and Joel McCrea. Stanwyck and the other Hollywood figures in town for the premiere stayed at the Hotel Fontenelle. The local paper reported that the "candy girl" at the hotel, Marina Gugas, age thirteen, and her younger sister had waited for hours to meet Miss Stanwyck. When the Hollywood star's entourage swept through the hotel lobby and directly into the elevator, the two young girls were crushed. A reporter found them crying. The next day, he told Miss Stanwyck about the two and said she replied that she would be happy to meet them. The *Evening World-Herald* on April 29, 1939, had a front-page photograph of the star with her two adoring fans.[33]

Prominent politicians also stayed at the hotel, including President Harry S. Truman. However, Truman's favorite Eppley hotel was The Elms in Kansas City. He was staying at that hotel when he received the telegraph from Governor Thomas Dewey congratulating him on winning the presidency in the 1948 election. He considered The Elms his "lucky" hotel, and Truman and Eppley became friends.[34] John and Jacqueline Kennedy stayed at the Hotel Fontenelle while he campaigned for the presidency in

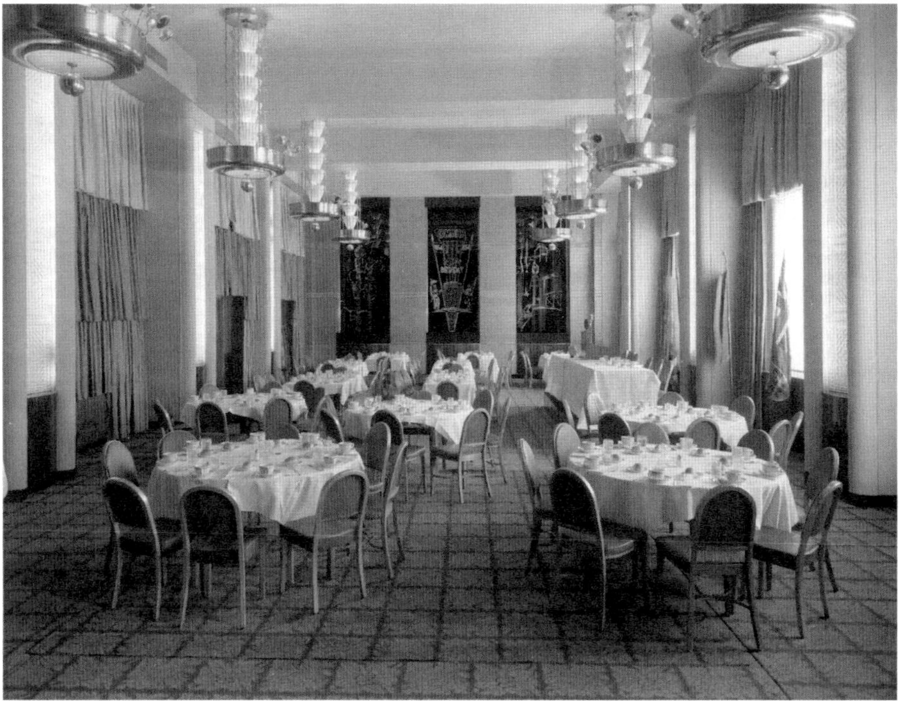

Generations of Omahans came to the Hotel Fontenelle to dine and dance in the Bombay–Black Mirror Room. In addition to music, entertainment over the years also included melodramas and other types of short plays. *Courtesy of the Durham Museum Photo Archives.*

1960. Senator Robert Kennedy headquartered his Nebraska presidential campaign office there in 1968.

Eppley did not just bank on celebrity guests. He also frequently upgraded the hotel's facilities, even during the Great Depression. In 1937, he created the Bombay–Black Mirror Room, a restaurant-bar facility. The project cost $60,000 and resulted in "a room adorned with black mirrors and subtlety illuminated by a system of diffused multicolored lighting."[35] The facility proved very popular during World War II. Seventy years later, members of the 504th Bomb Group—in town for a reunion and whose motto was "Omaha One More Time"—remembered traveling seventy-five miles from their training base in Fairmont, Nebraska, to visit "the classy Hotel Fontenelle."[36] For years after the war, Eppley ran a small advertisement almost daily in the local newspaper highlighting the entertainment available in the Bombay–Black Mirror Room.

Eppley suffered a stroke in May 1955 and a second one in September. In May 1956, he sold his chain of nineteen hotels to the Sheraton Corporation for $30 million. He continued to live in the Hotel Fontenelle in his suite, room 517. His health failed steadily thereafter, and on October 14, 1958, he died in his home at the hotel.[37]

The Sheraton Corporation operated the hotel as the Sheraton-Fontenelle until 1968, when it sold the lease to the Wellington Associates. In August 1970, a new Hilton hotel opened downtown, built on the site of the old post office. There had been many arguments made that downtown Omaha needed a second major hotel. However, just a few months later, on February 28, 1971, the Hotel Fontenelle closed its doors.

The article announcing the closing of the hotel noted that it had become "a little frayed around the edges." The elevator operator stated that the lights and buzzers didn't always work. And the reporter described the marble steps leading up to the mezzanine as "worn thin and loose in some places." Although the new owners had promised to "bring it back to what it should be," in February 1971, they "didn't want all this publicity" when closing the facility.[38]

The hotel still had two permanent residents when it closed. Mabel Gillespie Arehart, a widow and former newspaper reporter, had moved into the hotel in 1967. She hoped it was still salvageable, as she believed that "a lot of people have a place in their hearts for the Fontenelle." Grey Sterling had lived in the hotel since arriving in Omaha in 1965. He was less concerned with his move, saying he had adjusted to his new apartment within a couple of hours.[39]

The Hotel Fontenelle sat empty for many years. In 1973, two former employees returned to the vacant and decaying building and were interviewed by a local reporter. Former bell captain Leon Mutz remembered "when the Black Mirror Room was filled with well-dressed patrons, when silver glinted on spotless tablecloths and when the soft, rhythmic music of Art Randall and his Royal Fontenelle Orchestra lured patrons from cuisine to the dance floor nightly." Victor L. Spencer, another longtime employee, remembered "days and weeks when most of the Fontenelle's 340 available rooms were occupied; when Kiwanis and Rotary Clubs had offices in the hotel, when the Black Mirror Room entertainment included ice shows and old fashioned dramas in addition to the Randall orchestra." As late as 1967, the hotel still functioned as the city's convention center, hosting sixty-four events that year. By 1973, however, the interior of the old hotel was in bad shape. "Peeling paint hangs like stalactites from ceilings. Paint chips and plaster litter some floors. The building has not been heated in winter or cooled in summer and resulting condensation has eroded much of its former splendor."[40] And problems continued as, six years to the day the hotel closed, a five-alarm fire gutted the top three floors.[41]

Over the years, several local owners, including former mayor Eugene Leahy, hoped to redevelop the structure. However, the city condemned it in 1976. In 1979, a local developer spoke of plans to revamp it as a hotel or office space. But when Leon Mutz, who had toured the building in 1973, was asked if he would like to tour the building again, he replied he would rather not: "I think I'd just as well not see it."[42] In early January 1983, the city began demolition on the building. For many years thereafter, the site sat vacant, used as a parking lot.

OMAHA ATHLETIC CLUB

In 2000, Robert Putnam's book *Bowling Alone* attracted a great deal of attention. The work examines the ways in which America had transformed from a nation of "joiners" to one in which traditional forms of civic engagement and social connectedness—membership in civic organizations, clubs and even bowling leagues—were eroding.[43] In many ways, the Omaha Athletic Club suffered a fate similar to many of the organizations highlighted in Putnam's book. The club's membership peaked in the 1950s and early 1960s, only to erode dramatically starting in the mid-1960s, leading to its closure in 1970. The club had suffered setbacks in the past, closing temporarily between 1933 and 1936. But when its doors closed on September 4, 1970, this time it was permanent. The club's building—designed by John Latenser—had served as a center for recreation, club meetings and dining. Members and employees lived in apartments on the upper floors of the building. Several plans for reviving the building failed, and it was demolished in February 1992.

Planning for the creation of an Omaha Athletic Club—both an organization and a building—began in 1915 and was fully underway by spring 1916. A number of prominent Omaha businessmen, including George Brandeis, formed an organizing committee and began recruiting members. They promised a club building that would include such amenities as locker rooms, a barbershop, a gymnasium, a swimming pool on one of the upper floors, a running track and tennis courts. The new Omaha Athletic Club would also be a residential club, with members living in small apartments on the top floors. Initially, sixty-one original members declared they wanted rooms reserved for themselves in the new building. Organizers hoped to have at least 1,500 total members before beginning construction.[44]

On March 18, 1917, the local newspaper featured an image of the proposed new building on the north side of Douglas Street, between Seventeenth and Eighteenth Streets, and stated that construction of the eight-story building would cost approximately $400,000.[45] Construction began even as the United States entered World War I in April 1917. Though the club leaders hoped to open as early as May 1918, the war did slow construction, and the opening was pushed back to October and then November 1918.[46] At the same time, the local newspaper reported on labor issues—which also impeded construction of the new club—and the flu epidemic that was sweeping much of the world in 1918. It was the latter that would mark a first early challenge for the Omaha Athletic Club.

The leadership of the Omaha Athletic Club finally settled on December 12 and December 14 as the dates for events marking the gala opening of their new facility. The club would open to the public on December 12, and the members would enjoy a formal dinner on December 14.[47] Articles announcing the opening ceremonies appeared in both the sports pages and the society pages of the newspaper. Readers of the newspaper in early December 1918, however, would also have been aware of the mounting deaths from the flu epidemic—twenty-two on one day, sixteen on another. On the same page announcing that theaters would sell seats only in alternate rows in order to deal with the crisis, the Omaha Athletic Club announced that it would postpone its public opening, though the dinner for members would still go forward.[48] In fact, the club had to postpone the public opening of the club "indefinitely," until the flu epidemic abated.[49]

Though the group lost the opportunity to showcase its new home to the public due to the epidemic, the local newspaper continued to highlight the building's offerings. One feature that particularly caught the attention of the local media was the so-called Silent Room. A short article, accompanied by a number of cartoon drawings, explained its workings. Described, somewhat redundantly, as a "bedizened and decorated and dolled up parlor for men" where no sound was permitted, the newspaper speculated—tongue-in-cheek—that the Silent Room explained the large number of married men who had joined the Omaha Athletic Club. The article also added that no food was allowed in the room and that yawning was frowned upon. It concluded by stating, "You should go up there with your ear trumpet and learn something about the gentle art of whispering!"[50]

While the piece on the Silent Room poked fun at the club, the newspaper generally offered favorable reporting and over the years focused its coverage on the stories of the many athletic teams—swimming, golfing and tennis, among others—sponsored by the club. It also reported on the various civic organizations and clubs holding their meetings there. And it highlighted some of the service work the club hosted and members conducted, including offering swimming lessons to low-income children and swim therapy to polio victims.

Although the club and its building were regularly featured in articles in the local newspaper, the publicity could not help the organization overcome the impact of the Great Depression. The first sign of trouble came on February 26, 1933, a time that we now know was close to the absolute depth of the Great Depression as the nation still awaited the inauguration of its new president. On that date, the club announced that as of March 1, 1933, it would only accept cash. This applied to the "restaurant, barber shop, masseur department, card room, billiard room and other spots where service or merchandise is available." Noting that other athletic clubs in other cities had taken the same action, the club's president said that the board had deliberated for some time before making the decision but believed it was in the best interest of the organization.[51] The real reason for the club moving to an all-cash operation became apparent on March 2, when it was announced that the club had gone into receivership. Club president Frank McDevitt stated that the club would close unless it could sign up 350 new members by May 15, as membership had slipped in the past two years from 1,000 to 400. Apparently, the club did not meet that deadline, as a May 20 article noted that the "directors of the closed Omaha Athletic Club" had signed over all assets to creditors. Club members hoped that the local chamber of commerce might step in to lease the building or speculated that it could be converted into an apartment-hotel.[52] Neither plan came to fruition, however, and the club's building remained closed until late 1936.

Finally, in September 1936, John C. Allgaier, who (later with his son) managed the club from 1936 to 1963 and who purchased it outright in 1941, announced plans for a restructured organization that would reopen the facility. And by the end of the year, he had succeeded, as the club formally reopened in late December 1936 with a membership of six hundred.[53]

The Omaha Athletic Club continued as a place of meetings, banquets, wedding receptions and sports. Allgaier, though, found other ways to augment the club's income: slot machines. For the most part, gambling was illegal in Nebraska. Nonetheless, a major civic organization, AK-SAR-BEN, was known for its racetrack. And any number of private clubs operated slot machines through the 1940s. The machines in the basement of the Omaha Athletic Club received a good deal of probably unwanted attention with the arrest of Hershel Blackwell, a thief who targeted slot machines. He and four accomplices were arrested at the Omaha Athletic Club. Blackwell, already well known to police and notorious for his many arrests with no convictions, also managed to avoid jail in Nebraska as he and his accomplices posted bond and skipped town.[54] The news of the slot machines did not escape public scrutiny. However, the police commissioner had noted earlier in the year that he made it a "policy" to allow private clubs to operate "30 to 40 cash payout slot machines," as he viewed them as private property.[55] He also noted that the clubs paid a fifty-dollar federal tax on the machines each year. Though not all city officials agreed with the police commissioner's policy, slot machines remained a feature at local private clubs, including the Omaha Athletic Club, throughout the war years.

Members recalled later that the slots were extremely important to the financial health of the club. Reminiscing in 1992, longtime member dentist Dr. Emery LaPorte noted, "Boy they were busy....Allgaier used to tell me that he put way $75,000 a month [from the machines]." Another former club member, Frank Wear, recalled, "Slot machines helped subsidize the club....The old men would sit there in a chair and go to sleep and the women would be pulling the slot handles." He further speculated that local authorities turned a blind eye, as there were "a lot of important people at the club."[56]

VIP members or no, local officials finally cracked down on the illegal machines in 1949. In what had to remind at least some locals of a scene from the movie *Casablanca*, the city's acting mayor expressed "shock" at the idea of gambling in private clubs around the city. J.C. Allgaier denied any knowledge that slots operated at the Omaha Athletic Club or at the Happy Hollow Country Club, where he served as secretary-treasurer. The police chief promised swift action.[57] About a month later, the city's morals squad seized ten gambling machines (eight slot machines and two machines that dispensed cigarettes as the prize) from the club and arrested Allgaier for possession of gambling fixtures.[58]

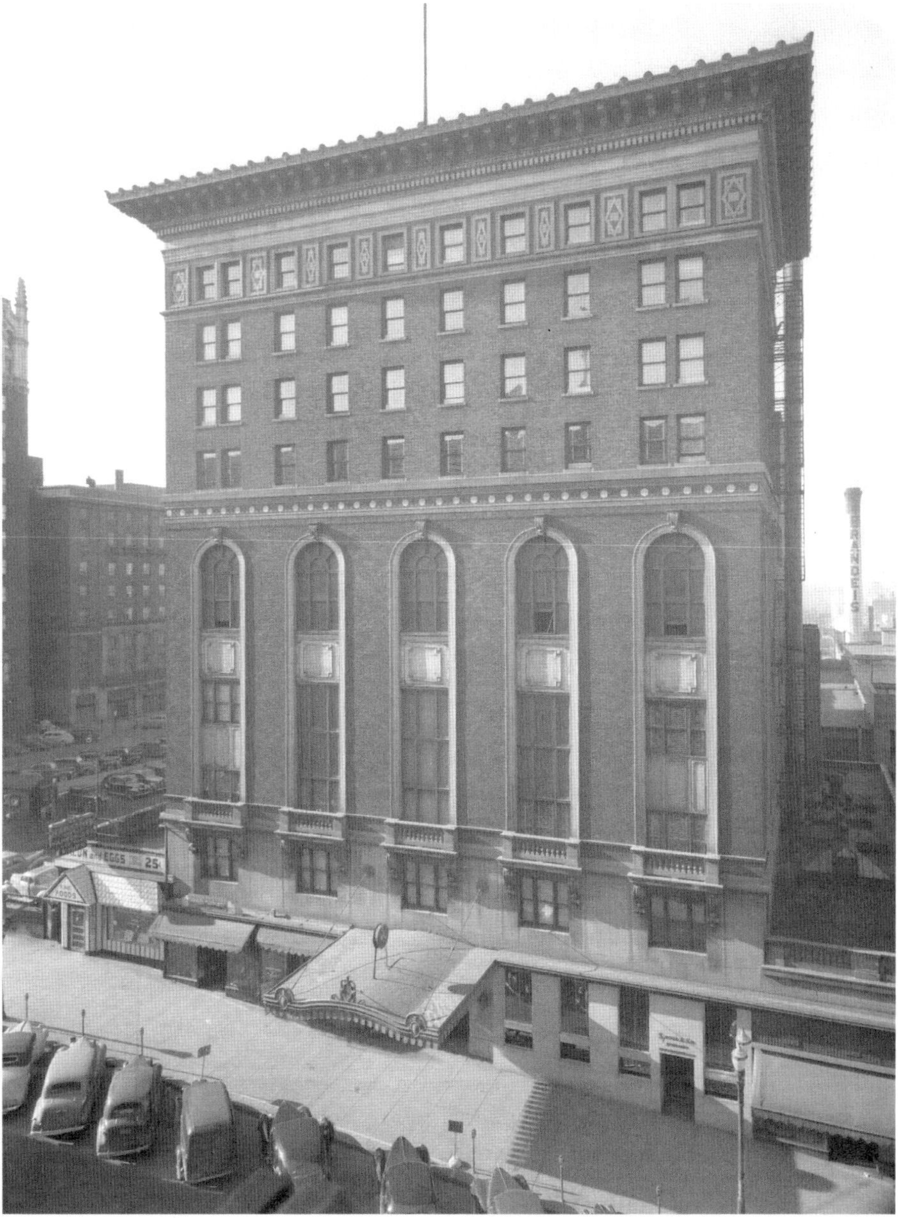

Generations of Omahans also came to the Omaha Athletic Club to dine, swim, bowl, play tennis and even gamble. *Courtesy of the Durham Museum Photo Archives.*

The charges against Allgaier were serious, carrying fines of $300 to $500 and up to two years in prison. The club also faced fines of up to $500.[59] The case dragged on for more than a year. Allgaier finally faced trial in January 1951. In other court action, the state's attorney general also sought an injunction prohibiting any type of gambling at the club.[60] In the end, Allgaier pleaded guilty to a misdemeanor charge and was fined $500.[61] The court battles did not seem to hurt the Omaha Athletic Club or its owner. Between the raid in 1949 and the trial in early 1951, the newspaper continued to report stories on civic organization meetings, wedding receptions, fundraisers and other society events at the club, along with Allgaier's success on the golf course and his many leisure trips.

Allgaier and his son continued to own and manage the club through 1963. On March 15, 1963, Larry Myers, a partner in the club with the Allgaiers, announced its sale to two real estate investors, A.W. Fulton and William Levey. The article did not include the sale price, nor did it give any sense of what would happen to the club under the new ownership, but it did state that the club building had been considered one of the city's "show places."[62] After Allgaier purchased the club, he managed to grow its membership. Soon after Fulton and Levey took over, however, the club's membership began to shrink. In 1963, membership stood at 2,000. By 1970, it had dropped to between 1,200 and 1,300. The club's attorney noted that private clubs all over the country were also experiencing eroding memberships, noting, "Young people are not interested in joining, perhaps because of the transient nature of today's population." On September 4, 1970, the Omaha Athletic Club closed its doors.[63]

The general population may or may not have been transient in 1970, but there was nothing transient about many of the employees of the Omaha Athletic Club, as a good number had worked there for twenty or thirty years at the time of its closing. In fact, the club's chef, Rinaldo "Reno" Sibilia, started work on December 14, 1918. Except for the three years it closed during the Depression, he worked for the club from that date until September 4, 1970. In an interview, the seventy-four-year-old chef told the newspaper that it was perhaps time for him to take a rest. He told the reporter that he would miss the people. He thought the Omaha Athletic Club was something that Omaha needed, as it was more than an "impersonal hotel" and for the people who lived there, it "was more like a home."[64]

Although there was some early hope that the club might be sold and reopened, as had happened in the 1930s, this time the closure was permanent. The building sat vacant for a number of years. In 1977, the

Federal Reserve Bank bought the Omaha Athletic Club building, as well as the adjacent Baird Building. Bank officials noted that the purchase came at a time when the bank was planning an expansion of its facility, located on the same downtown block, between Seventeenth and Eighteenth Streets, Dodge and Douglas Streets. Though there was speculation that the Federal Reserve would build a new facility on that site, the Federal Reserve Board initially rejected plans for a new building. Five years later, in 1983, the Federal Reserve finalized plans for a new building, not at its original site but at Twenty-Second and Farnam. At the same time, the Federal Reserve announced plans to sell its other properties in downtown, including the Omaha Athletic Club.[65]

A property development firm entered an agreement to purchase the property in 1988, having announced plans to construct a $20 million hotel-office complex on the site. However, by 1989, the company had defaulted on the loan, and the Federal Reserve announced plans to sell the property at auction. In early 1992, though, the Federal Reserve still owned the property and in February hired Anderson Excavating and Wrecking Company to demolish the building. The implosion came at 8:40 a.m. on a Sunday morning that same month, and in eight seconds, it became a pile of rubble.[66] Today, the site of the Omaha Athletic Club, as well as the Hotel Fontenelle, is the home of the Roman L. Hruska U.S. Courthouse, completed in 2000.

CHAPTER 2

PEONY PARK AND AK-SAR-BEN

ONCE PLACES OF SUBURBAN LEISURE—SWALLOWED UP BY COMPETITION AND URBAN GROWTH

Peony Park

In the early twentieth century, automobile enthusiasts promoted the improvement of roads throughout the United States. One of the most important of these early roads was the Lincoln Highway, one of the nation's first transcontinental highways. Although the route changed over time, in the 1910s, travelers on the part of the highway that wound its way through Omaha would pass by what is now Seventy-Eighth and Cass Streets near J.F. and Carl Rosenfield's peony farm. Across from that farm, Joseph Malec Sr. and his brothers purchased ten acres of land along the Papio Creek. There they opened a refreshment stand in 1916. In 1919, they replaced the stand with a filling station and added a restaurant—the Peony Inn—in 1921. As automobile traffic along the highway grew, the brothers added a ballroom in 1923 and a swimming pool in 1926, and the original ten acres grew to twenty-four (and eventually to forty).[67] By the 1930s, the Malec brothers' Peony Park was well on its way to replacing Krug Park—which closed in 1940—as Omaha's most popular amusement park.

As common with the stories of many local landmarks, Peony Park experienced its share of early difficulties, including both fire and recurrent floods. The 1923 ballroom burned down in 1925. But within months, the brothers had replaced it with a new brick ballroom an advertisement touted as "The Largest and Most Beautiful Dance Pavilion in the City."[68] Flooding of the Papio Creek, which ran along the east side of the park, in 1932 and

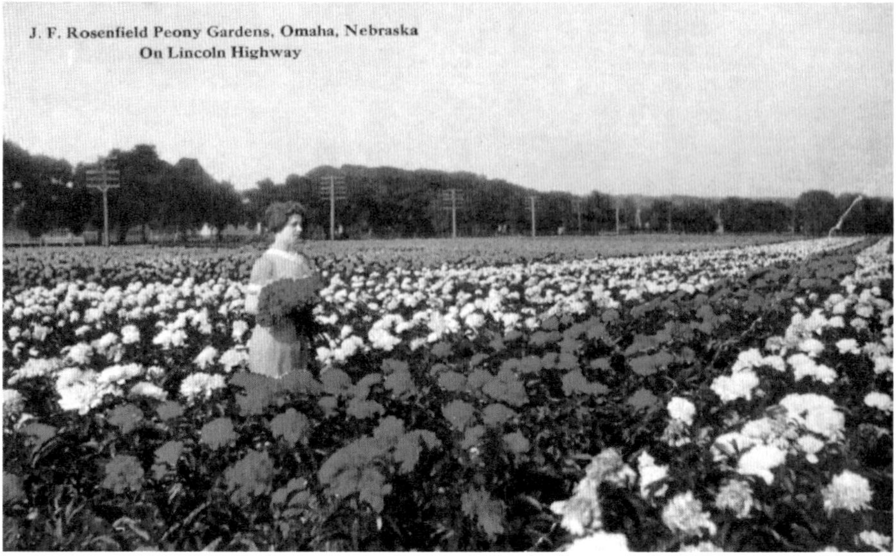

Peony Park was named for the peony farm across the road. *Courtesy of the Omaha Public Library Collection.*

1943 did extensive damage. In both floods, the swimming pool was heavily damaged and had to shut down. In 1932, the August flood, which set a record for the most rainfall in a twelve-hour period, resulted in the pool being closed for the rest of the season. However, the dance hall, though closed during the flood, reopened immediately after. The damage from the 1943 flood was more extensive. In fact, the local newspaper reported that the park received the heaviest damage from that event. Joseph Malec Sr. estimated his repair costs at $50,000 and thought the park would be closed for at least thirty days. The water came up fast, and Malec reported he "could hear trees and fences snapping as the water came down." Several feet of water covered the park, including the terrace surrounding the dance hall. Oddly, the dance floor itself was undamaged. Even though the dance floor sat forty inches below the surrounding terrace, Malec could only guess "that the flood came and went so fast that the water didn't have time to get to the center of the dance floor before it began receding." The flood happened on June 2, and the park reopened on Friday, June 25, though the pool stayed closed until Sunday, June 27. Malec credited the young people working for him: "We had to depend mostly on youngsters and they gave us a fast and swell job. We got the park ready a week ahead of the time scheduled."[69] Not surprisingly, Malec became a strong advocate for Papio Creek flood control.

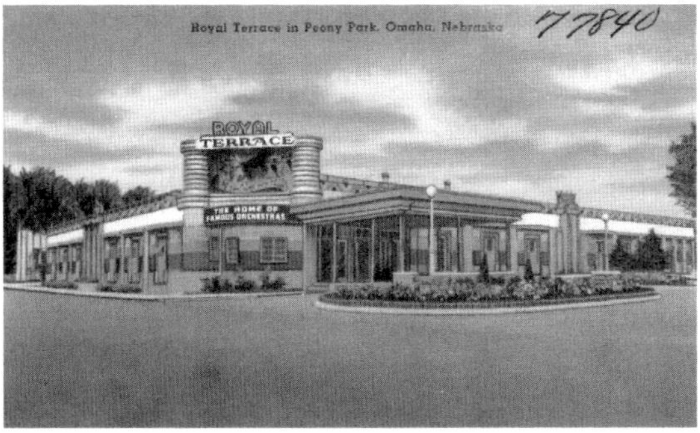

The Royal Grove opened in the 1930s. "Royal Terrace in Peony Park, Omaha, Nebraska." Card, 1930. *Digital Commonwealth, ark.digitalcommonwealth.org/ark:/50959/xs55mk81j (accessed August 19, 2016).*

From the 1930s through most of the 1950s, Peony Park was best known for its ballroom and swimming pool. In the late 1950s, however, the park added a number of "kiddie rides" aimed at the younger crowd. Charles Malec, from the second generation of the family to own and operate the park, designed the new attractions. An advertisement in March 1958 listed the features of the new section of the park. They included "a helicopter, new to the Midwest; railroad train complete with station, trestle, and long tunnel; merry-go-round; ferris wheel; miniature roller coaster; Turnpike auto ride; and pump carts." Malec traveled to other popular parks, including Disneyland and Santa Claus Land, while researching his design. Wonderland also included an eighteen-hole Around the World miniature golf course and a storybook playground with "The Old Woman in the Shoe, big enough for her many children, Willie the Whale spouting water, the little red school house complete with bell but no teacher, wicked dragon, castles, bridges, waterfalls, rockets, and space ships." Early stories about the addition noted that the Malecs were investing more than $100,000 in these park improvements. At opening, the newspaper cited a figure of "close to $200,000." Whatever the cost, Wonderland opened on May 30, 1958.[70]

That same year, the City of Omaha annexed Peony Park and the surrounding neighborhood. When the Malecs first opened their refreshment stand across from the peony farm, the area was described as "five miles west of the city." As late as 1940, the City of Omaha zoned the land just west of Peony Park for agricultural uses, but by the late 1950s, suburban housing and commercial developments surrounded the facility. Though many homeowners in the area resisted, the owners of Peony Park did not fight the annexation. At the time it officially became part of Omaha, though located in a part of town considered a "fringe area," Peony Park was on its way to being surrounded by urban development.[71] Two years later, for example, the nearby Crossroad Shopping Center opened, catering to the residents of the growing western areas of Omaha.

Peony Park hit its peak as an amusement park in the late 1950s through the early 1970s. Dancing and live music, though, did much to help keep the park open through the early 1990s. As noted, the park's first ballroom opened in 1923. In 1934, the Malecs added an outdoor concert area known as the Royal Grove. A full-page advertisement on June 6, 1934, announced that the Royal Grove would open the following day and described it as having "10,000 Sq. Ft. of Dance Floor, 2,250 Seating Capacity, Covers Over Four Acres." The new Royal Grove offered dancing every night except Monday. It also offered space for picnics and group outings.[72] In the late 1960s, Joe Malec Sr. remembered the "golden age" of the Peony Park music facilities as the ten years before World War II. During that decade, as many as 3,400 people would dance "to the music of Glenn Miller, the Dorseys, Henry James, Eddie Howard, Guy Lombardo, Jan Garber, Leo Pieper, Sammy Kaye, Duke Ellington, Cab Calloway and Lawrence Welk." Bands would arrive on Mondays and play all week. Between Memorial Day and Labor Day, most music and dancing took place "under the stars" in the Royal Grove. When the weather was cooler (or wetter), they moved inside to the ballroom. By the late 1960s, the park offered dancing and music only two nights a week. However, other events, such as company and alumni picnics, kept the facilities busy at least five days a week.[73]

Old-fashioned ballroom dancing continued at Peony Park until the ballroom closed in 1994. For decades, the Midwest Ballroom Dancers Association held regular Tuesday night dances. It was on a Wednesday night, however, that the park hosted the last ballroom dance. "A whirl of corsages, glittery dresses, dark suits and silver hair brought an era to a

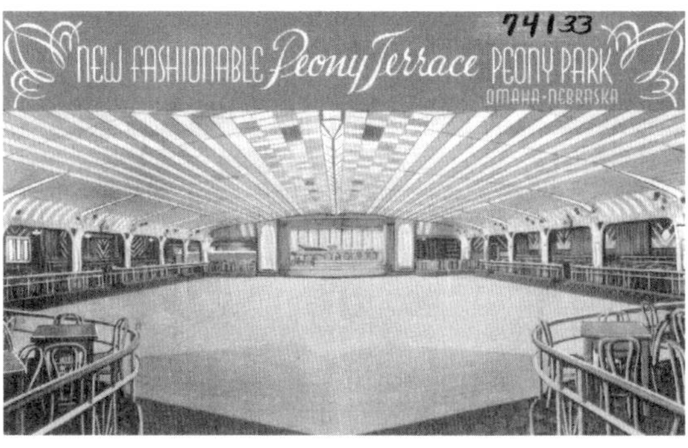

Couples could dance at Peony Park year-round under cover in the Terrace Ballroom. "New fashionable Peony Terrace, Peony Park, Omaha, Nebraska." Card, 1930. *Digital Commonwealth, ark.digitalcommonwealth.org/ark:/50959/xs55mk89r (accessed August 19, 2016).*

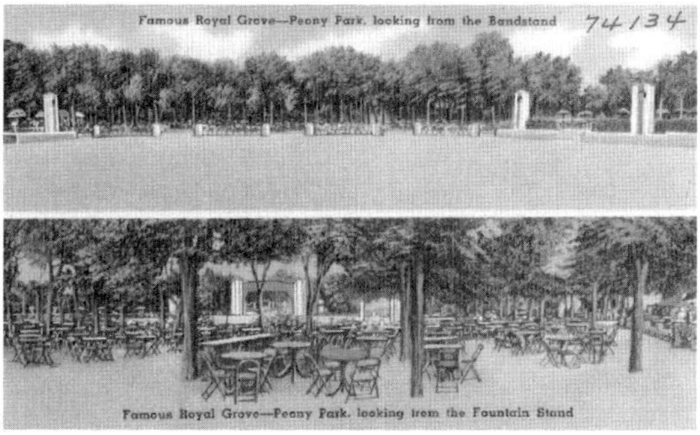

During spring and summer, couples could dance "under the stars." "Famous Royal Grove—Peony Park, looking from the bandstand." Card, 1930. *Digital Commonwealth, ark.digitalcommonwealth.org/ark:/50959/xs55mk719 (accessed August 19, 2016).*

close Wednesday night as older park patrons paid their last respects to the 75-year-old amusement park's ballroom." Tommy Dorsey's orchestra played as couples—young and old—danced "The Last Waltz." Lorvey Schwinck remembered, "In the last 13 years I've been to almost every Tuesday night dance here unless I was out of town." He and his wife both declared they would miss the "landmark" park. Another couple, Leo and Dorothy Dwyer, drove from Bartlett, Nebraska, "to spend a final evening in the ballroom, where they danced when they were 'younger.'" And Ray Sena, who remembered his high school prom, called the shuttering of the ballroom "a real sad day for Omaha, I think."[74]

Old-time swing bands weren't the only musical acts at Peony Park, however. The owners also catered to the younger crowd. Peony Park's Grove and Ballroom were "bigger than a club and smaller than an arena," a size that attracted many up-and-coming bands. Parents also felt safe sending their teenagers to the park. Omaha's young people, thus, witnessed early performances by such groups as Pearl Jam, the Red Hot Chili Peppers, Nirvana and Faith No More.[75]

The other major feature of the park was its swimming pool. In 1926, the Malecs transformed a small pond on the property into a swimming pool unlike any other in Omaha. The pool, the largest in the city, covered nearly a square block. Sand covered the bottom—reported as the only sand-bottomed artificial pool in the country—and created a beach-like area surrounding it. Several artesian wells supplied the water, which kept pool temperatures at a chilly fifty degrees. Though made to look "natural," the pool was created with a great deal of modern technology. As Joe Malec Sr. described: "Six hundred thousand gallons of fresh water are added daily and we have a pumping system that sends 450 gallons of water into the pool every minute. In addition, we used the most modern sterilization system, which treats all the water at the Peony Park pool and kills all dangerous microbes. We have

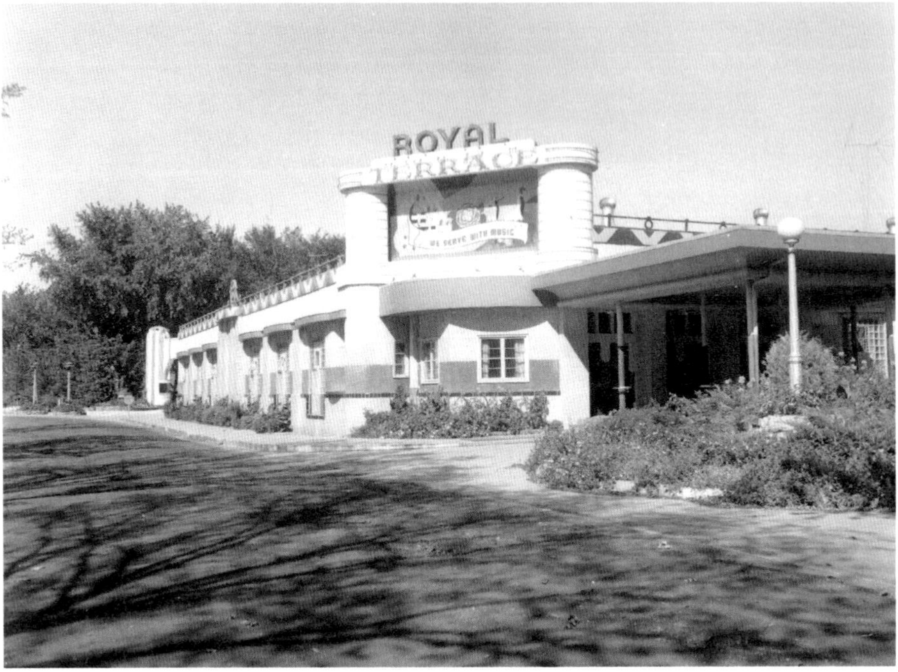

The Royal Grove remained popular until the end. *Courtesy of the Durham Museum Photo Archives.*

three large fountains which constantly hydrate all water coming into the pool and adds the right amount of hydrogen."[76]

The Malecs' policy about who could swim in the pool, however, left a legacy of bitterness for many Omahans. In 1954, in something of a prelude to a larger crisis in the early 1960s, Peony Park officials refused to allow two young African American males to participate in the Peony Park Open Swimming and Diving Championship. The two had qualified for the meet, and their entry forms had been accepted. However, when they showed up for the competition, park officials turned them away. The NAACP filed suit on behalf of Bob Biddle and Leonard Hawkins. The case went to court, where an attorney representing the park pleaded "no defense" and the court issued a fifty-dollar fine. The attorney blamed the incident on a "misunderstanding"—implying that the entries should not have been accepted in the first place.[77]

The incident in 1954 did not result in a change in policy. In 1963, however, similar events resulted in widespread protests and the eventual desegregation of the pool. In early June, an enlisted airman from nearby Offutt Air Force

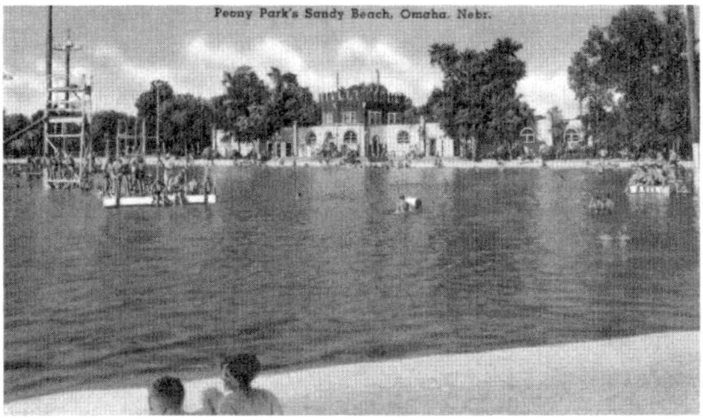

Also popular was the Peony Park pool. "Peony Park's Sandy Beach, Omaha, Nebr." Card, 1930. *Digital Commonwealth, ark.digitalcommonwealth.org/ark:/50959/xs55mk698 (accessed August 19, 2016).*

Base sought admission to the Peony Park pool. He was denied because of his race. Frederick Winthrop took his complaint to the City of Omaha, and on June 14, the city attorney filed charges against Peony Park for violating the state's civil rights law. The small story about the incident was buried at the bottom right of page two of the newspaper. A few weeks later, the paper reported that the city prosecutor would not accept a second complaint—this one made by United States Air Force captain Michael King—until the courts had decided the case involving Winthrop.[78]

By mid-July, actions to end racial discrimination at the park went beyond filing formal complaints. On Saturday, July 13, "three carload of Negros" were refused admittance to Peony Park. Charles Malec said that although African Americans had been admitted to some areas of the park in the past, he decided to turn them back "until everything settles down." Malec justified his actions, noting that the park was "flooded" with calls about integrating the pool and claimed that "25 of every 26 callers" opposed integration. The young people mounting the demonstrations did not stop. They returned on Sunday, and Malec responded by closing the park. Over one hundred people participated in the peaceful demonstrations that day.[79] Malec reopened the park on Monday but closed it again on Tuesday, July 16, the same day the governor visited Omaha for a firsthand look at the city's racial problems. Although Governor Frank B. Morrison declared that the demonstrations would only "inflame people and prey upon their passion," after he held talks with the county officials, the county attorney decided to file charges based on Captain King's complaint in the U.S. District Court.[80]

The Malecs then hatched a plan to open the park as a "members-only" private club. Patrons coming to the park would pay the admission price and receive a one-day membership in the club. The employees of the park would determine who could receive a membership card.[81] Young members

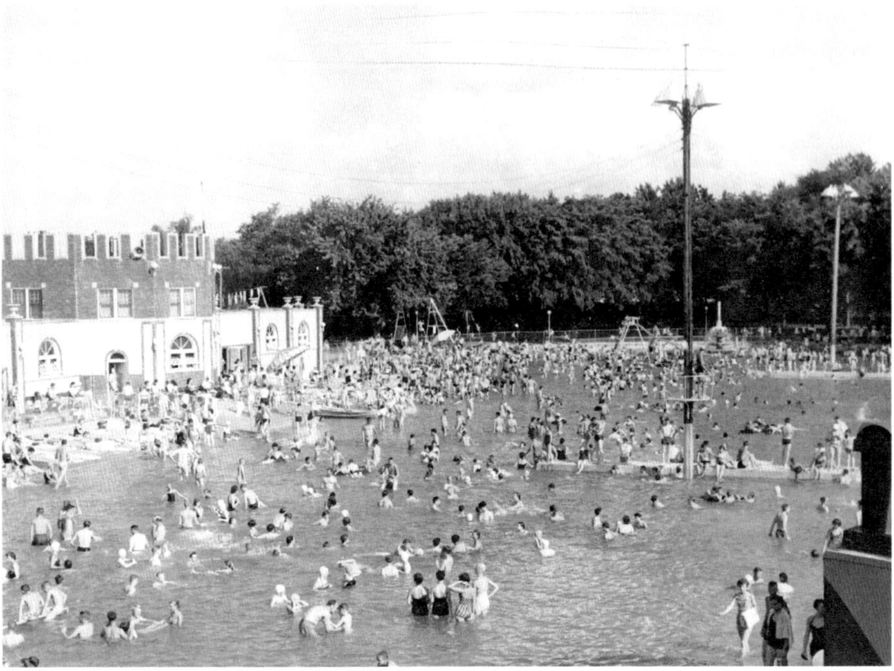

The swimming pool was popular but also a source a great controversy in the 1950s and 1960s. *Courtesy of the Durham Museum Photo Archives.*

of the NAACP, including Leonard West, a junior at the University of Omaha, and Terry Edwards, a recent graduate of Tech High School, strongly criticized the action. On the other hand, Mayor James Dworek viewed it as a solution to the problem.[82] A few days after reopening as a private club, Joseph Malec Sr. said that both blacks and whites had been denied membership, though all had been offered membership forms. Apparently, only individuals well known to park employees were granted memberships. Others, both black and white, had to wait while their membership applications were scrutinized. Malec estimated that the park had between five hundred and six hundred membership applications yet to process. By the middle of the second week, however, Malec announced that the park was looking for a way to open as a "Park for All," though for the time being it would continue to operate as a private club.[83]

In the meantime, the cases against the park continued through the courts. And pressure came from other quarters as well. Below a front-page article detailing Department of Defense plans to place "off limits" places that practiced racial discrimination, the local newspaper reported that approximately ten young African Americans had been seen swimming in the Peony Park pool on July 26. Others followed, including Leonard West and fellow University of Omaha student Herbert Rhodes. Both were also members of the Catholic Interracial Council.[84] The case involving Captain King received national attention, including an article in *Look* magazine. Shortly after the pool closed for the season, Omaha's Municipal Court fined Peony Park twenty-five dollars in the case involving Frederick Winthrop, and the U.S. District Court imposed the same fine in the case involving Captain King.[85] As far as can be determined from the local newspaper, the park and pool opened as desegregated facilities with little fuss or fanfare for the 1964 season.

Years later, as Peony Park prepared to close, Herbert Rhodes, who served as chairman of the Omaha Human Relations Board, remembered the summer of 1963 and was "shedding no tears" for the park. He remembered being turned away from the park, saying, "That kind of rejection does hurt." Rhodes also remembered that the park's actions angered many whites, including his Cathedral High School teammate Dan McGinn, a major-league pitcher. Rhodes concluded, "The policy was not supported by the people of Omaha. It wasn't something that Omaha citizens accepted as part of the culture." Still, Rhodes only visited the pool once as an adult. His children used the park—and, as the local newspaper concluded, that "was why he sought entrance in the first place."[86]

Peony Park continued to grow and change well into the 1970s. In 1970, the Malecs convinced the City of Omaha to repeal its ban on roller coasters—a ban put in place after four people died in a coaster accident at Krug Park in 1930. Attendance soared, with the number of paid admissions doubling between 1971 and 1972 and increasing 40 and 38 percent in 1973 and 1974, respectively. Even during a cool 1975, attendance climbed 15 percent. But competition was also growing. A Worlds of Fun opened in Kansas City and Adventureland in Des Moines. Further, Peony Park had no room to expand. In 1978, a thirteen-year-old boy, Neil Tetzlaff, fell to his death from a ride in the park when his restraint came unlatched. The accident highlighted the fact that Peony Park employed primarily teenagers to operate the rides. (The author's brother, a Creighton Prep High School student, worked at the park that summer.)[87]

Competition, lack of room for expansion and bad press all contributed to the gradual decline in the park's fortunes. Debt from an expansion project in the 1980s resulted in bankruptcy in 1992. Although several groups floated plans to preserve the park, Peony Park closed on March 31, 1994. A couple weeks later, the park's remaining assets—everything from amusement rides to the chandeliers in the old ballroom—sold at auction.[88]

Once the park closed, several visions for reuse of the property came into conflict. Cass Street Properties envisioned a retail development including a supermarket and other stores along Cass Street with apartments planned for the northern part of the property, behind the retail area. Another group, Partners for a New Peony, tried to raise money to purchase the site and develop it into a city park. A third group, Peony Partners, envisioned a Victorian theme park on the site. That group stated, "We believe that the Peony Park site is a part of Omaha's folklore and cultural heritage and, along with Henry Doorly Zoo, the Central Park [Gene Leahy] Mall and Rosenblatt Stadium, will add significantly to our quality of life, our identify as a community and our ability to attract new business." Though the park proponents hoped the new mayor, Hal Daub, would support the project, the retail development won out.[89] What was once Peony Park is now a Hy-Vee Food Store surrounded by a number of restaurants and shops. An apartment complex was built behind the Hy-Vee.

AK-SAR-BEN Racetrack and Coliseum

AK-SAR-BEN is Nebraska spelled backward. It is also the name of a civic and philanthropic organization founded in 1895. For most of its history, the organization has supported agriculture (hosting livestock fairs and rodeos) and has awarded scholarships. For many in Omaha, however, it was best known for its racetrack, coliseum and annual coronation ball, in which a (male) local civic leader and the daughter of a prominent family are crowned the king and queen of the mythical kingdom of Quivera. Today, the organization still supports agriculture, awards scholarships and crowns its royalty. The racetrack and coliseum, however, are gone.

In March 1919, the organization purchased two hundred acres west of Sixtieth Street on West Center Street, a site that included the former grounds of the Nebraska State Fair and what would become the city's first airport. AK-SAR-BEN bought the property in order to build a horse racing track and exposition hall. The site already had the remains of a one-mile racetrack, constructed in 1898 but unused for many years. Work began on the new track in May and finished in early June. There was some urgency, as another local racing facility in the Benson area had recently closed and the horses and trainers needed a new home. Initially, AK-SAR-BEN moved the barns from the other track as a temporary measure. The organization hoped to have new barns completed within a few months.[90]

Though the track was ready for local horses and trainers in 1919, it did not open for racing until September 1920. On September 14, a day with what the local newspaper called "perfect weather," AK-SAR-BEN held opening ceremonies for the track and grandstand. The paper might have especially noted the weather that day, as in April, a small tornado had damaged the racetrack's grandstand while it was under construction. As a result, the grandstand had not yet been completed in September, but it was ready enough to host the ceremonies and the first races of the season. With the contractor still pouring concrete in the lower levels and putting the finishing touches on the roof, over 16,000 people came for the Thursday races—so many that they overflowed the grandstand (capacity 8,500). The facility was so crowded, in fact, that it delayed the airmail operations on the nearby field for several hours that day. The newspaper reported that the racing facility had cost $1 million and that an additional $1 million had been raised for its operation and upgrade.[91]

As noted, at the same time AK-SAR-BEN first hosted horse racing, the site also served as the home of Omaha's first airport. The United States Post Office began its experimental airmail service in 1918. By 1920, it was operating a transcontinental airmail route, and Omaha, already a center for mail-by-rail, became an important stop. To help secure its place on that first transcontinental airmail route, the chamber of commerce worked with AK-SAR-BEN to build a hangar on the property the group had purchased just the year before. Airmail operations began on May 15, 1920.[92] Soon the Omaha field played an important role in an early experiment to prove the value of the new airmail service.

Though Americans generally responded to aviation with great enthusiasm, the post office's airmail operations faced congressional opposition. To prove the value of the new service, the postmaster general devised a plan to fly the mail nonstop, day and night, both east and west across the transcontinental route. For both symbolic and political reasons, the postmaster general chose February 22, 1921 (Washington's birthday and ahead of the inauguration of President Harding), to conduct the experiment. Two planes left the East Coast and two planes left the West Coast. At all stops along the route, relay pilots and their planes awaited their turn. The effort soon ran into problems, as bad weather stopped both west-bound planes and one of the east-bound planes. The other east-bound plane, however, landed in North Platte,

Nebraska. Anxious to get started on the next leg of the journey, airmail pilot Jack Knight boarded his plane at 10:44 p.m. to carry mail between North Platte and Omaha. He landed in Omaha at 1:10 a.m., knowing that the pilot who was supposed to fly the next leg was stranded in Chicago. The experiment might have ended there, but Knight, who had never flown east of Omaha, nonetheless declared that he would fly the mail on to Chicago. Navigating with just a compass and a road map, Knight found his way through snow and freezing weather first to Iowa City and then to Chicago. At Chicago, two other pilots flew the mail on to New York. The post office, thanks to Jack Knight, had flown the mail across the country in thirty-three hours and twenty-one minutes—two days faster than the fastest train. Jack Knight and Omaha's AK-SAR-BEN airmail field had earned a spot in aviation history.[93]

By 1924, however, AK-SAR-BEN, which also had planned to build an exposition building on its property, notified the chamber of commerce that it wished to end the airmail operations. At the same time, the post office decided that the field was now too small to handle the mail and made plans to move its operations to Fort Crook (now Offutt Air Force Base), south of the city. Giving these events a note of finality, on June 22, 1924, a tornado destroyed the hangar and seven airplanes.[94] AK-SAR-BEN's role in Omaha's aviation history was over. A new chapter in the organization's history, though, was on the horizon.

Though AK-SAR-BEN very quickly raised the money for the new racetrack, it took a number of years for the group to raise the funds for the promised exposition building or coliseum. The organization finally announced the start of construction on the new coliseum and livestock pavilion in March 1928, less than a year after fire destroyed the organization's original headquarters—the Den—on North Twentieth Street. The start of construction coincided with a membership drive. The organization hoped to have four thousand members (a goal later raised to five thousand), each of whose names would be on a scroll placed in the cornerstone of the building. The group also planned additional livestock barns and an expansion of the racetrack's grandstand. Though the membership drive fell just short of its expanded goal, the cornerstone was laid on May 25, 1928.[95]

The Coliseum was ready for the annual coronation ball in October 1928. Unique to the ceremony that year, many former kings and queens participated. The orchestra from the Hotel Fontenelle provided the music. Miss Emma Creighton Nash assumed the crown as queen of Quivera (an announcement that rated a front-page banner headline), while Walter W.

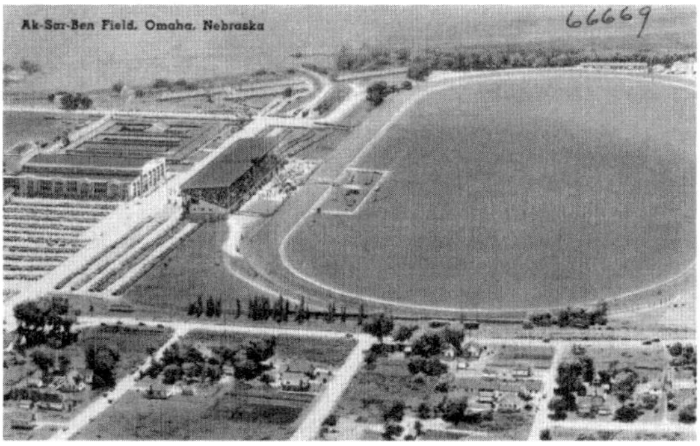

This early postcard shows how the neighborhood around the AK-SAR-BEN Racetrack and Coliseum was just beginning to develop. "Ak-Sar-Ben Field, Omaha, Nebraska." Card, 1930. *Digital Commonwealth, ark.digitalcommonwealth.org/ark:/50959/xs55mk299 (accessed August 19, 2016).*

Head was crowned as king. Soldiers from Fort Omaha participated as an honor guard. The ceremony started late, as a traffic jam slowed the arrival of the more than ten thousand reported attendees. Those attending also had to contend with mud, as a recent rain had turned the not yet completed grounds around the building into a quagmire. Despite the problems, the newspaper concluded that the ceremony provided a "fitting opening of the organization's new home."[96]

The Coliseum also opened in time for the organization's first annual horse and livestock show on November 5, 1928. An event described as "the biggest thing that Omaha has attempted since the Trans-Mississippi exposition" occupied the Coliseum space that a few weeks earlier had hosted the coronation ball. The new event came at the end of what was a banner year for the organization. The racetrack also had its biggest year to date in 1928.[97] The next year, however, the State of Nebraska banned horse racing, a ban that stayed in place until 1935.

A few years after the resumption of horse racing, AK-SAR-BEN brought a new sport to Omaha: professional ice hockey. The organization had installed a temporary ice rink in the Coliseum as part of its annual horse and livestock show in 1938, which also featured an ice follies show. The following year, citing a long-standing local demand for a facility to host hockey, ice shows and public ice-skating, the organization's board of governors approved the installation of a more permanent ice rink in the Coliseum. It would be available from November 1 through April 15 every year. Progress was swift. AK-SAR-BEN signed the agreement for the installation of the ice rink in September, and by October, the city had a team from the American Hockey Association. The first season for the Omaha Knights opened on the new ice on November 15, 1939.[98]

Even non-hockey fans could enjoy the new facility. Many skating enthusiasts formed ice-skating clubs. But the ice was open not just for clubs and other organizations but for "people in all walks of life." Except on days when hockey games were scheduled, the ice was open for public skating in both a morning and evening session. An adult ticket cost forty cents; children could skate for twenty-five cents. Season tickets for the rink were also available. The manager estimated that "thousands" would enjoy the new facility.[99] (The author learned to ice-skate at the rink in the late 1960s.)

World War II interrupted horse racing, hockey and the coronation ceremony. The U.S. Army Transport Command set up operations on the AK-SAR-BEN grounds in 1942 and stayed for the duration. Racing resumed in 1945, as did hockey. During the 1945–46 season, the team had a young player named Gordie Howe playing right wing. Another elite athlete, 1935 Triple Crown winner Omaha, also arrived at AK-SAR-BEN after World War II. In 1950, Omaha moved to a horse farm near Nebraska City and would frequently travel to the AK-SAR-BEN track, where children could have their photos taken sitting on the fabled horse. When the horse died in 1959, he was buried in a Circle of Champions on the AK-SAR-BEN grounds.[100]

The AK-SAR-BEN organization and its facilities flourished after World War II. People came from throughout Omaha and surrounding states for the racetrack, the agricultural programs (including an annual rodeo) and the ice rink (for ice hockey and for recreational skating). Members were treated to annual "members-only" shows at the Coliseum that featured some of the biggest names in show business, including Mario Lanza, Red Skelton, Pat Boone, Jimmy Dean, Jerry Lewis, Victor Borge, Wayne Newton, Bill Cosby, Sammy Davis Jr., Rita Moreno, Rosemary Clooney, Shirley Jones, Carole Channing, the Lawrence Welk Orchestra and the Charlie Daniels Band.

AK-SAR-BEN's more suburban location and plenty of parking helped it attract and accommodate large crowds. To keep people coming, however, the organization financed a major renovation of the facilities in 1965–66. The organization resurfaced the racetrack and added a new isolation barn (required under state law for the testing of horses) in time for the racing season.[101] The Coliseum received the most visible and extensive changes. The largest complaints most people had when attending events involved the many posts supporting the ceiling that obstructed sightlines. As part of a $2 million project, a fewer number of larger pillars and new roof trusses replaced the original posts. Outside, a new steel façade covered the old brick walls. The Coliseum also received a new state-of-the-art sound system. Further, a new banquet hall, with seating for up to 1,800, occupied an old passageway between the Coliseum and the racetrack's grandstand. AK-

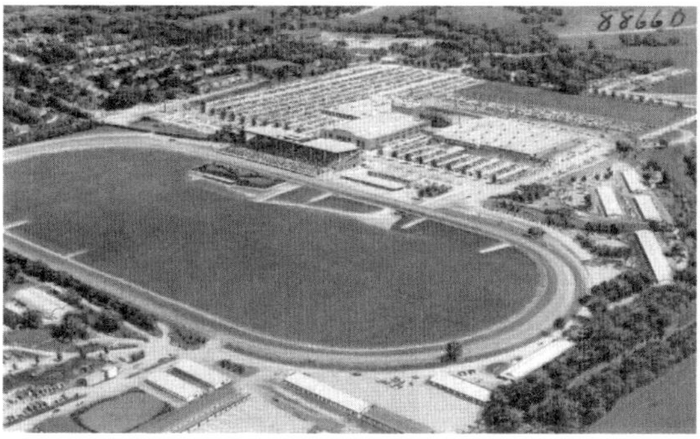

The AK-SAR-BEN Racetrack and Coliseum hosted nationally recognized horse races as well as livestock shows and big-name entertainment; the later postcard shows more neighborhood development around the complex. "Aerial view of Ak-Sar-Ben field." Card, 1930. *Digital Commonwealth, ark.digitalcommonwealth.org/ ark:/50959/xs55mm43b (accessed August 19, 2016).*

SAR-BEN announced that the new banquet hall was available for use by outside groups, but under strict conditions. Groups renting the facility must be nonprofits "of religious, agricultural, educational, horticultural, public or civic welfare nature." And the groups could not use the facility for any event meant to earn them a profit, such as a fundraiser. AK-SAR-BEN held an elaborate dedication ceremony for the new facilities on April 20, 1966.[102]

AK-SAR-BEN's good fortune continued well into the 1970s and early 1980s. However, just as with Peony Park, matters changed in the mid-1980s. Fifty years after racing resumed, in 1985 AK-SAR-BEN's racetrack had it best year—in just one day, 31,630 racing fans bet $3.5 million. The track averaged $1.8 million per day during that racing season. It ranked among the top ten racetracks in the country. People came from throughout the Midwest to bet and enjoy the races, as well as the fare at local steakhouses. As many as 800 people worked at the track during the race season.[103] The following year, however, a dog racing track opened across the Missouri River in Council Bluffs, Iowa. In 1991, the first casinos opened in Iowa. As other forms of gambling became available, the horse racetrack—in Omaha as elsewhere—suffered.[104]

As attendance fell and losses mounted, AK-SAR-BEN looked to sell its property. In April 1992, Douglas County agreed to purchase the facilities—racetrack and Coliseum included—for $25 million. As part of the sale, the county created two public corporations: Douglas Racing Corp. (RaceCo) to run the track and Douglas Recreation Corp. (NonRaceCo or RecCo) to operate the rest of the property, including the Coliseum. County Commissioner Mike Albert, who also served as president of the Douglas Racing Corp., hoped the county could use the property "as a tourist attraction and as a site for meetings and conventions," much as the Knights of AK-SAR-BEN had. Revenue from racing and keno games (added in the early 1990s) would finance the purchase. However, in June 1992, the county learned that the AK-SAR-BEN facilities had lost $2.1 million in the year before the sale, including $1.7 million from the racetrack—far more than had been expected.[105]

Despite efforts on the part of the county, the racetrack continued to decline. In 1996, before the start of the racing season, RaceCo voted to end live races at the track. Kenny Rosen, the chairman of RaceCo, stated, "No one feels worse about this than I do." Clare Duda, chairman of the county board, concluded, "It's not a happy day....I don't enjoy seeing racing die. But there's no way we can justify having a live meet. We have no choice." Finding ways to finance the rest of the facilities also proved a challenge as the non-racing operations, particularly the Coliseum, also lost money.[106]

Local race fans and former employees of the track all lamented the track's closure. Red Albertson, a former horse trainer, had a long history with the track. "I come here just about every day. I've been coming here better than 50 years. There were a lot of good years, especially in the late '70s and the '80s. There were rows and rows of buses in the parking lot, from Kansas City, Des Moines, all over." Ray Price grew up near the track. His mother was an avid bettor, attending "most days from the late 1930s until she died in 1974." Even though Price was not the race fan his mother was, he would still miss the atmosphere around the track during race season. He recalled that parked cars along the streets surrounding AK-SAR-BEN often slowed traffic to a crawl. He didn't mind the traffic, as "it meant something exciting was happening." He also recalled the excitement around the finish line at the track. "Everybody rushed down there to watch the race. There was always a lot of electricity in the crowd."[107]

No sooner had the decision been made to close the racetrack than numerous ideas bubbled up for what to do with the AK-SAR-BEN property. The Omaha Lancers hockey team wanted a new arena. The mayor and the chancellor of the University of Nebraska–Omaha (UNO) envisioned an expanded UNO campus. The Knights themselves envisioned a conference center or other forms of community development. And although there were still some determined to salvage live horse racing at the track, events moved quickly toward a radical transformation of the property.[108]

If AK-SAR-BEN, with its emphasis on agriculture, represented Omaha's history and heritage, First Data Resources, a credit and bank card processing company, in many ways represented the city's future. In May 1996, First Data proposed a $40 million development on the AK-SAR-BEN property that would also leave room for UNO. First Data suggested that its expansion would create two thousand jobs. UNO planned to create a new College of Information Science and Technology, whose graduates would fill many of those jobs. At the time, First Data was Omaha's largest private employer. Community leaders revealed plans for the new high-tech office park and campus in June 1996. The plans involved a complicated transaction in which the county property would be turned over to a new Ak-Sar-Ben Future Trust. The Knights of AK-SAR-BEN would forgive the county's outstanding debt ($10 million) from the original sale in 1986. The Knights and other bondholders would also surrender their bonds to the new trust. First Data Resources would then pay $10 million to the trust for 120 acres (later 140 acres) of land. It would keep half for its new facilities and donate the other half to UNO. The over 200 acres remaining—including the Coliseum—would remain with the new trust. The county board approved the concept in June 1996 and in January 1997 agreed to the final sale of the property.[109] Demolition of the race facilities (not including the grandstand) began in April 1997. First Data opened its new center in 1998, and UNO opened the Peter Kiewit Information Science, Technology and Engineering Institute in 1999.

Attention soon shifted from the racetrack to the Coliseum. As construction began on the First Data and UNO facilities, the Ak-Sar-Ben Future Trust promised to keep the Coliseum open. One of the major tenants of the building was Omaha's minor-league hockey team, the Omaha Lancers. The Lancers came to Omaha in 1986, eleven years after the Knights left town. Proving that Omaha was a hockey town, the team had 210 straight sold-out games going into the 1997 season. However, that season also marked the start of new competition for the Lancers, as UNO fielded an ice hockey team that would play in Omaha's downtown Civic Auditorium.[110] Within two years, the future of the Coliseum and the Lancers was in doubt.

In 1999, Ak-Sar-Ben Future Trust announced that it was losing more than $1 million per year. Without an infusion of funds, the trust would have to close down the remaining facilities on the AK-SAR-BEN property within four years. In 2002, the Lancers moved to a new arena in Council Bluffs, Iowa. Lancers owner Ted Baer said the team had no alternative, as owners of the AK-SAR-BEN Coliseum failed to renovate the facility: "I never thought the Lancers would out-live Ak-Sar-Ben." Motto McLean, who played for the Knights from 1947 to 1951 and from 1960 to 1961, declared, "You're taking away history, which is a really sad thing." The Coliseum also hosted the last livestock show and rodeo that year.[111]

Demolition on the Coliseum, grandstand and all other remaining building began in mid-2004. At the time, there was no clear strategy for the future of the property. However, a year later, the Ak-Sar-Ben Future Trust announced plans for extensive development of the remaining acres. The so-called Aksarben Village was designed to mimic "pre–World War II neighborhoods that grew up near college campuses." The Shoppes at Ak-Sar-Ben opened in 2005, and in 2007, officials broke ground on the "$200 million worth of apartments, row houses, entertainment venues, office and commercial buildings and…hotel" that would replace the old racetrack and Coliseum.[112]

Tucked away in a corner of Stinson Park, part of the new Aksarben Village, is the grave marker for Omaha, the Triple Crown winner, buried near the grandstands in 1959. It stands as a reminder of the glory days of AK-SAR-BEN and horse racing in Nebraska.

CHAPTER 3

JOBBERS CANYON, THE OMAHA STOCKYARDS AND PACKING PLANTS

OMAHA'S BLUE-COLLAR HERITAGE, OR WHEN $3.18 AN HOUR WAS A GOOD WAGE

JOBBERS CANYON

Jack Kerouac's novel *On the Road* begins with Sal Paradise embarking on a cross-country trip from New York City to San Francisco. Early on in the book, Sal describes crossing the bridge (most likely the AK-SAR-BEN Bridge) from Council Bluffs, Iowa, into Omaha, where he saw his first cowboy "walking along the bleak walls of the wholesale meat warehouses."[113] The buildings in Omaha's riverfront wholesale district near the bridge did not house meat companies, but companies engaged in the agricultural equipment industry and the wholesale food industry were prominent. It was not known as Jobbers Canyon when Sal Paradise made his fictional cross-country trip in 1947. In fact, it was not known as Jobbers Canyon until shortly before it ceased to exist. It was, however, a significant part of Omaha's riverfront and labor heritage.

Jobbers Canyon was a collection of mostly six- to eight-story brick buildings occupying a district from Eighth to Tenth Streets, Farnam to Jackson Streets. Constructed primarily in the early twentieth century, the buildings marked Omaha's emergence as a major commerce center. The six-block area was not the entirety of the city's wholesale district—that also included what is now known as the Old Market Historic District and the Omaha Railroad and Commerce Historic District. Many other early downtown warehouse buildings also survive. Jobbers Canyon, though, was

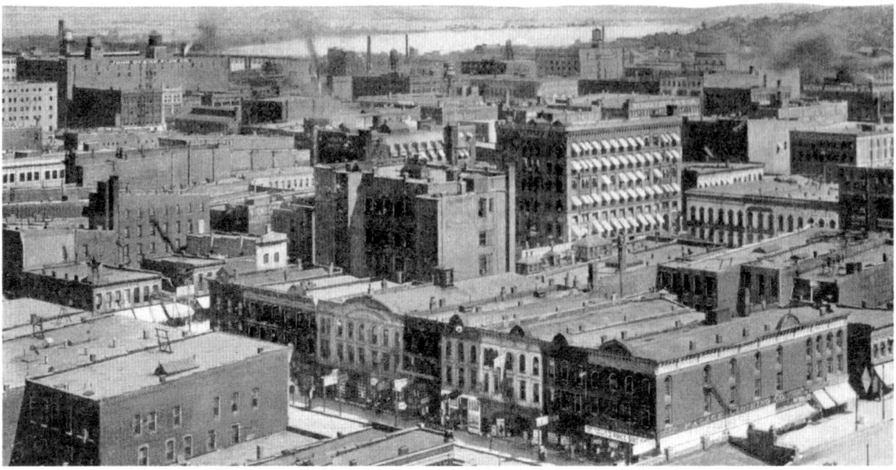

Jobbers Canyon was part of Omaha's large warehouse and wholesale district. In this postcard image, Jobbers Canyon is in the upper left side, surrounding the John Deere Building. *Courtesy of the Omaha Public Library Collection.*

an area with a significant concentration of such buildings—most of which were still in use as warehouses in the late 1980s.

The Jobbers Canyon Historic District included twenty-two "contributing buildings" and four "non-contributing buildings," to use the language of the form submitted to the National Register of Historic Places. The contributing buildings, many designed by prominent local architects, included:

Rector and Wilhelmy Company Building (one of the oldest, with the original section of the building built in 1889)—hardware
American Radiator Company Building (designed by John Latenser, built 1905)
Lindsay Brothers/New Idea Building (1890)—farm machinery
Kingman Implement Company (U.S. Tire Building) (1900)
Crane Company Building (Nogg Brothers Paper Company) (1905)
Fairbanks, Morse and Company (1907)—industrial and agricultural equipment
John Deere Plow Company Building (1908)
John Day Company Buildings (1892)—hardware and contractor supplies
U.S. Supply Building (1906)—steam, water and plumbing supplies
Dempster Building (John Latenser, 1902)—agricultural supplies

Lee-Coit-Andreesen Hardware Company Building (1916)
H.J. Lee Warehouse Building (1900)—hardware
Harding Cream Company Building (1904)
Carpenter Paper Company Building (John Latenser, 1906)
Omaha Cold Storage Building (1913)
Creighton Block (1905)—dry goods
J.I. Case Plow Works Building (George Prinz, 1913)—agricultural implements
Trimble Brothers Building (John Latenser, 1920)—fruit and vegetable commission merchants

According to the nomination form, wholesale jobbing—buying directly from a manufacturer and selling to store owners—became a significant business activity in the United States starting in the 1850s with the construction of the first railroads. The railroads made the transportation of goods both faster and more dependable. At first, most wholesale jobbers located along the East Coast. By the 1870s, however, with the expansion of the nation's railroad network, wholesale jobbers had set up in interior cities such as Cincinnati, Chicago and St. Louis. The first jobbers arrived in Omaha in the 1880s. Enjoying a brief period of growth during that decade, the trade suffered dramatically in the depression of the early 1890s. The return of prosperity late in that decade benefited Omaha tremendously. Omaha civic leaders also aggressively sought to build the city's reputation as an important trade center. Most of the buildings in Jobbers Canyon were built in response to those developments. Local companies or investors built some of the buildings; others were constructed as branch offices for national corporations.[114]

By the late 1980s, the area was still the site of warehouse and wholesale operations. Wright and Wilhemy, a hardware wholesaler, ranked as one of the oldest businesses in the city. Founded in 1871 in Nebraska City as Larson and Wilhemy (which became Rector and Wilhemy in 1876), the company moved to Omaha in 1883 and built its warehouse on the riverfront in 1889. The company then doubled the warehouse's capacity in 1905, three years after it became Wright and Wilhemy. In 1987, a company spokesperson said the warehouse currently had an inventory of over thirty thousand items and employed seventy-five people. Perhaps the most active business in the area was Omaha Cold Storage, "said to have once been the largest cold storage house between Chicago and the Pacific Coast." It still operated in its 1913 building at 809 Farnam Street. The company also operated out of the Lee-Coit-Andreesen Hardware Company building, the

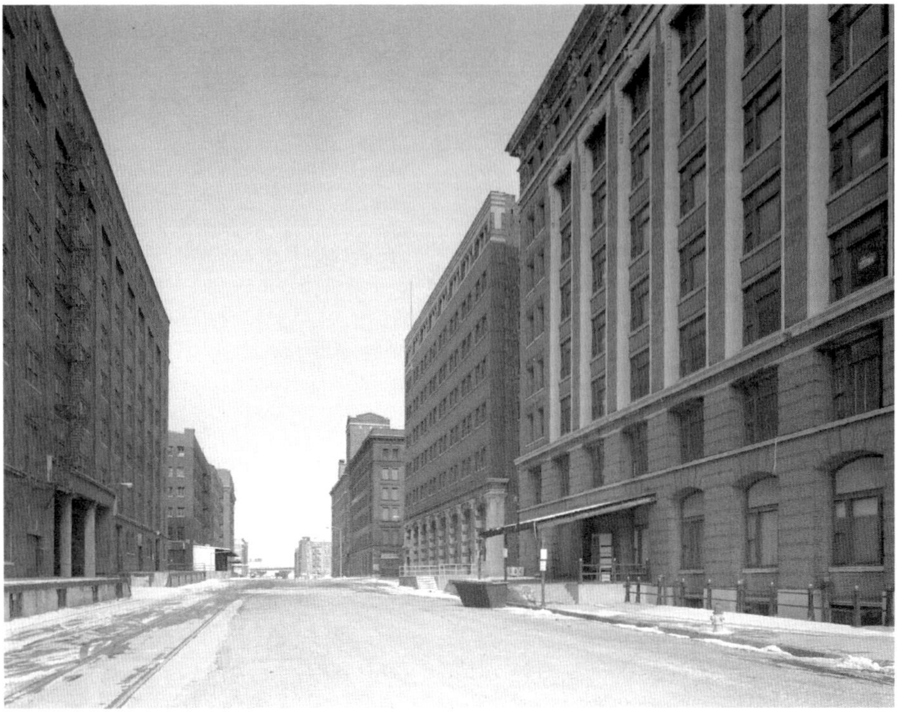

Jobbers Canyon was so named because the rows of warehouses along the narrow streets of the district gave it a canyon-like appearance. *Courtesy of City of Omaha, Landmarks Heritage Preservation Commission, Meyer Collection.*

Harding Cream Company Building and the H.J. Lee Warehouse building. Nogg Brothers Paper Company purchased the Crane Company building in 1966. Crane had used the building as a warehouse distribution center, focusing on products such as "wrought iron pipe; boiler tubes; all types of gas, water and stem supplies; plumbing materials; hydraulic machinery; mill, elevator and machinery supplies; metals; belting, and hose." Nogg also used the building as a warehouse. In addition to Nogg Brothers, Jobbers Canyon was also the home of the Carpenter Paper Company, which opened Omaha's first paper warehouse in 1886. It built its headquarters building in 1906. In 1987, the building, "said to be the first reinforced concrete building built west of Chicago," held "several million dollars of inventory."[115] John Deere Plow Company also continued to use its building as a warehouse, as did the John Day Company.

Other buildings had already found new uses. The McKesson Robbins Building (the last remaining building of what was once a three-building complex—see below) was already undergoing renovation to transform it into an apartment building. Renovation was also underway at the New Idea Building at 902 Jackson Street. The building had originally housed a wholesale supplier of medicine, liquor and paint supplies. In 1927, the New Idea Spreader Company (later the New Idea Farm Equipment Company) purchased the building. New Idea distributed farm equipment manufactured in Ohio. Lindsay Brothers, also a wholesale distributer of farm equipment as well as plumbing and heating supplies, purchased the building in 1958. That company occupied the building until 1985. In the late 1980s, the renovated building housed apartments and a management and organization consulting firm. The Creighton Building—which had housed a number of businesses, including the Byrne and Hammer Dry Goods Company, Tootle-Campbell Dry Goods Company and Appleman-Robbinson—was said to be "the most ornate in the district." It was also undergoing renovation while serving as the headquarters for the Cibola Corporation, a company founded by "former Enron executives and former Mayor Mike Boyle." And the U.S. Supply Building housed the Metropolitan Arts Council.[116]

The Omaha City Planning Department submitted the form for Historic District designation in September 1986. The National Register added the Jobbers Canyon District in early 1987. Almost immediately, Omaha civic leaders and ConAgra, a Fortune 500 company then headquartered in the city, began discussions concerning a new headquarters for the company. The proposed site was the new Jobbers Canyon Historic District.

Civic leaders were quite anxious to keep ConAgra in Omaha. In 1986, Enron—the former Northern Natural Gas Company—moved its headquarters from near downtown Omaha to Houston, Texas. Though local leaders attempted to put a good spin on the news, they also strongly criticized the business climate (read city and state tax structure) as being unfriendly to corporations. So, when ConAgra threatened to leave, civic leaders determined to do whatever was necessary to keep it in Omaha. First, they supported a tax reform bill in the Nebraska state legislature. Second, they supported the demolition of Jobbers Canyon to make room for a new suburban-style headquarters campus for the company. The Omaha Development Foundation, an arm of the chamber of commerce, began negotiations with building owners in 1987. ConAgra announced plans for its new headquarters on January 5, 1988. Douglas County also agreed to build a thirty-acre park on part of the site. The companies located in Jobbers Canyon generally supported the effort, though they did push back against the initial buy-out offers. The city's historic preservation community, on the

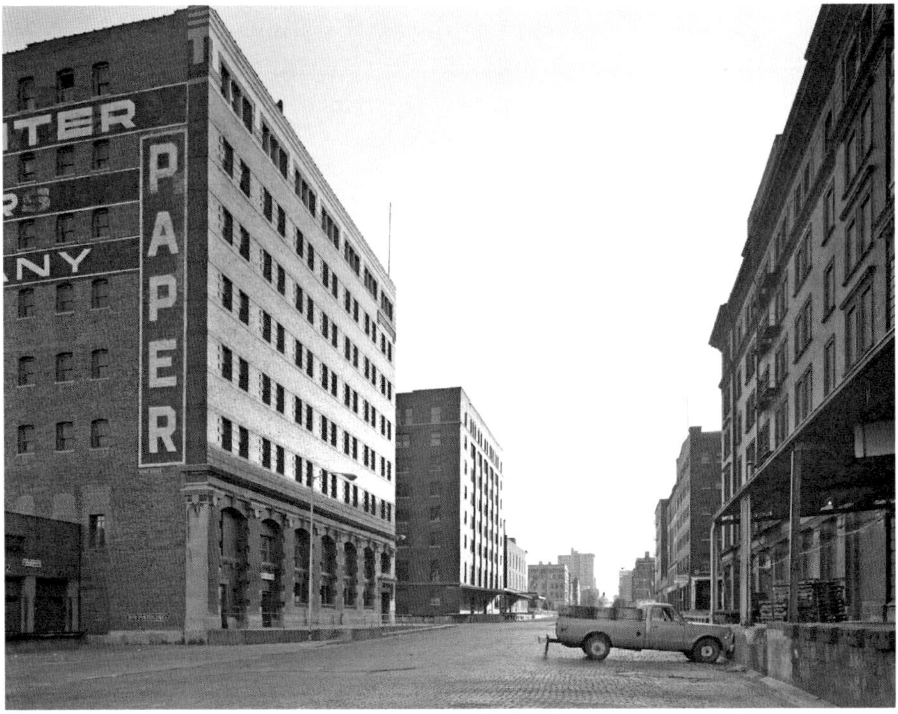

Many of the streets in the Jobbers Canyon District were still paved with bricks. *Courtesy of City of Omaha, Landmarks Heritage Preservation Commission, Meyer Collection.*

other hand, mounted a determined resistance. Court fights continued even as demolition began. Despite all efforts, Jobbers Canyon was gone by the summer of 1989.[117] It is still the largest historic district ever demolished.

Though the warehouse district disappeared, many of the businesses that operated in Jobbers Canyon survived (at least for a time)—though often far from the downtown. Carpenter Paper moved to a new warehouse facility it constructed at 52nd and F Streets. The new building was not as large as the one in Jobbers Canyon, but it had "much taller ceilings and [could] store more products," according to the vice president of operations. Nogg Paper also increased its storage space when it moved to a new warehouse on Abbott Drive, where it still operates as Nogg Chemical and Paper. The John Day Company moved to a new location near Abbott Drive as well. The company president stated that the new location would allow it to operate more efficiently. In Jobbers Canyon, the company operated out of three multistory buildings and had to use elevators to move products. The new

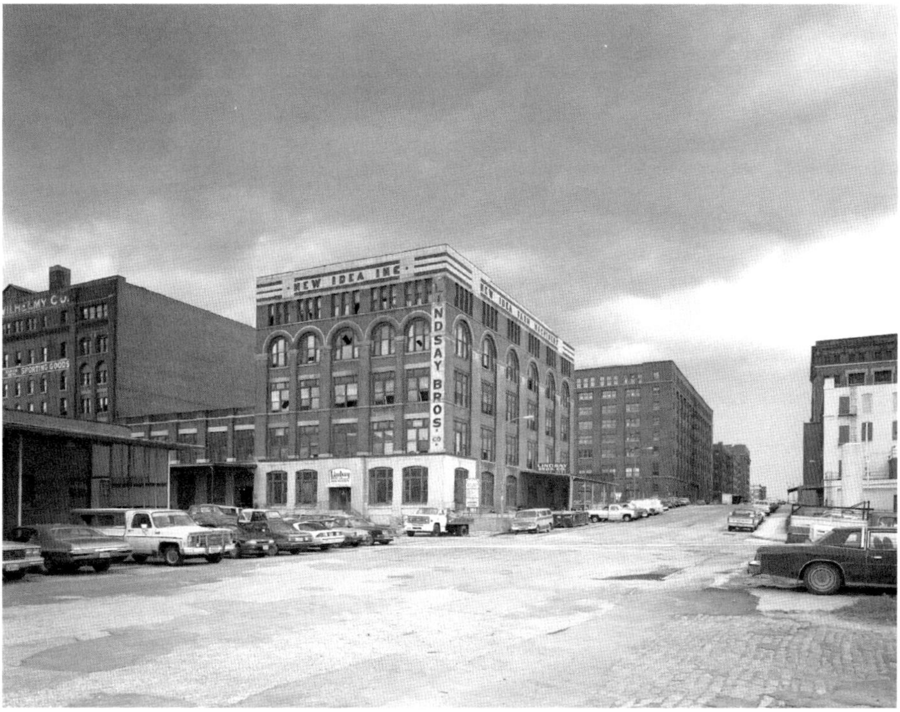

New Idea/Lindsay Brothers; some of the building had been converted to apartments. *Courtesy of City of Omaha, Landmarks Heritage Preservation Commission, Meyer Collection.*

location was on a single level. In 2016, it had three branch locations and employed approximately one hundred people. Both Nogg and John Day received relocation aid from the city. The Omaha Paper Company moved from 901 Jackson to 69th and L Streets, where it still operates. Wright and Wilhemy moved from the riverfront to a location in West Omaha at 111th and E Streets. The company had already constructed a warehouse at that location. Before moving all its operations to the new existing warehouse, the company built an addition that increased the total square footage to 106,500 feet. Even though the new facility was still a bit smaller than the company's Jobbers Canyon location, similar to Carpenter Paper, the taller ceilings actually gave it more cubic feet of storage space. Company president Warren Daasch declared, "We're very pleased with it." Cibola Corporation moved to offices at 110th and Q Streets. And Omaha Cold Storage moved to 5025 South 33rd Street—a location now listed as the former location of Omaha Cold Storage. At the time, however, the company was pleased with the move. The company president said the new facility, formerly B.C. Dressed Beef, was not only newer but better. Although smaller, it could still "handle the same volume of refrigerated materials." And best yet, the new building cost less than the $4.8 million the company received for its Jobbers Canyon properties.[118]

The original home of Omaha Cold Storage was not the only lost piece of Omaha's history associated with the company. Sometime after Omaha Cold Storage left downtown for South Thirty-Third Street, Sonja Henie's heart was also lost. The saga of Sonja Henie's heart began in early 1941. Barney Oldfield—a military officer and publicist, not the race car driver—received a request from Ray Gaynor, the advance man for the ice show coming to the AK-SAR-BEN Coliseum. Gaynor wanted Oldfield, who was working in army public relations at Fort Crook, to dream up a publicity stunt that would guarantee Sonja Henie would get her picture in the local newspaper. The show was scheduled for February 13, 1941. Oldfield contacted Julius Gagani at Omaha Cold Storage. He needed a one-hundred-pound block of ice. Gagani offered Oldfield a block that had been died blue-green and an ice

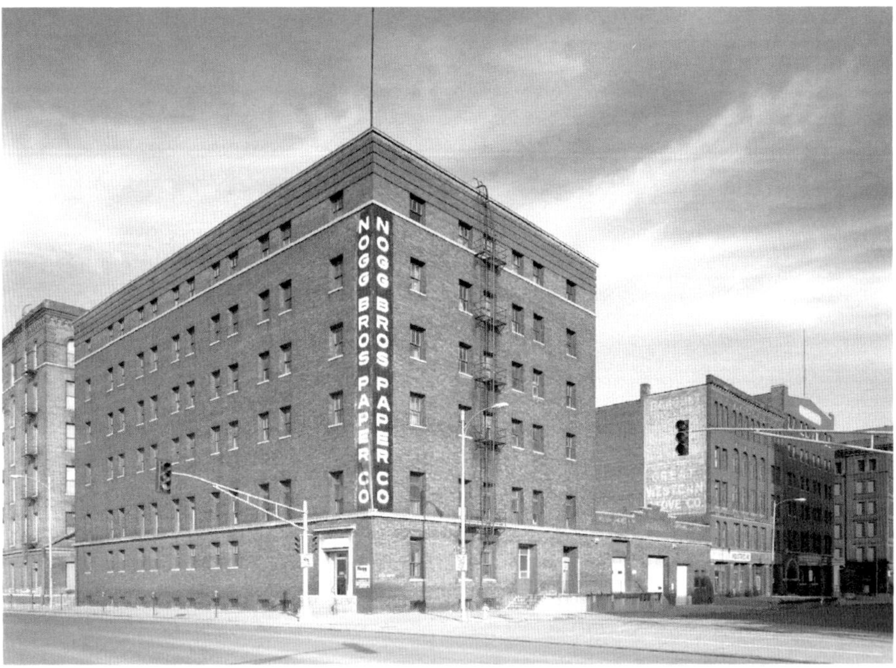

Nogg Brothers Paper Company. *Courtesy of City of Omaha, Landmarks Heritage Preservation Commission, Meyer Collection.*

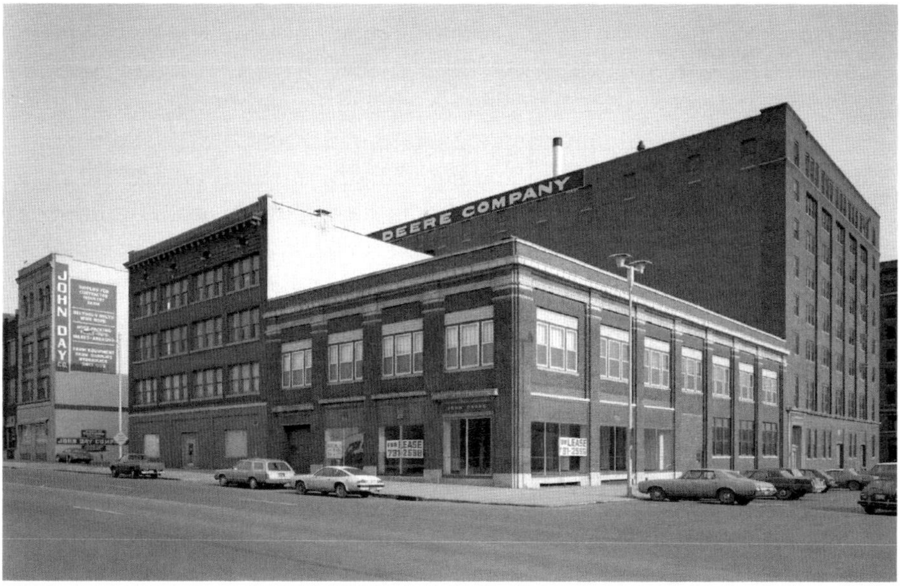

Another view of the John Deere Building. *Courtesy of City of Omaha, Landmarks Heritage Preservation Commission, Meyer Collection.*

pick, which Oldfield used to carve a heart—a nearly one-hundred-pound icy valentine heart for Miss Henie. Oldfield and some soldiers from Fort Crook loaded the heart into a truck and took it to the AK-SAR-BEN ice rink. They presented the heart to Miss Henie, who tried to autograph it with a hot nail. Unfortunately, the autograph attempt failed, and the heart was melting. Henie's photograph with the heart, though, did make the local paper. Oldfield promised Henie, "We're going to keep the valentine until you come back to Omaha some day." He returned the heart to Omaha Cold Storage, where it was placed in a box labeled "Sonja's valentine." Apparently, Henie never returned to Omaha and died in 1969. Oldfield placed a rose on the heart box after her death. He last returned to Omaha and saw the heart in 1991. But sometime after that, the heart disappeared. In 2003, the president of Omaha Cold Storage said, "It was here two to three years ago…But it is not here now. We have looked; it was either misplaced or it is just gone."[119]

Jobbers Canyon, in some ways, only existed for a few years—from its designation as a historic district to its demolition. The memory of Jobbers Canyon, what was lost with its demolition, has remained sharp in Omaha for the last quarter century. And once ConAgra announced that it was moving its headquarters from Omaha to Chicago in 2015, the debate over preservation versus progress received another airing. The move gained even more controversy when it was clear that the Merchandise Mart—a Chicago riverfront warehouse facility—would house the company's new headquarters. Omaha's preservation community responded, "The irony is incredible. Imagine…if they had kept those great warehouses, how cool and hip those spaces would have been." Elsewhere in the city, a number of projects were underway converting old warehouses and other commercial spaces to new uses. Boyd Jones Construction, for example, was involved with a $25 million renovation of the old Burlington mail terminal. And the Peter Kiewit Foundation was leading an initiative "to buy up old industrial properties north of Cuming Street to help establish an 'arts and trades' district for budding creative types. Leaders viewed that as a way to keep sharp talent in the city, in turn sharpening the city's competitive edge." Many wondered if Jobbers Canyon might have evolved into Omaha's own Merchandise Mart—now the home of both technology companies and startups. But as Kristin Gerber of Restoration Exchange Omaha concluded, "That's our history—you can never get it back."[120]

Architect Roger duRand has argued that Omaha's downtown redevelopment would have continued even without ConAgra's headquarters. DuRand worked on a plan that would have included Jobbers Canyon as a logical extension of the Old Market. It would have been part of a redevelopment project extending from the heart of the downtown to the riverfront. The "unique urban streetscape" of the canyon would have attracted residences, offices, shopping, entertainment and other uses to the area. In fact, redevelopment was already underway. "Investors had spent $1.7 million to put apartments in the New Idea building at 902 Jackson St." DuRand said that plans were underway for other buildings in the area: "They were useful buildings. They had hundreds of years of life left in them."

Former director of city planning Marty Shukert, on the other hand, argued that ConAgra's headquarters "played a large role in the renaissance of the downtown." He noted that the city gained "25 years of major corporate occupancy downtown. There was value just in that." He also said that the demolition of Jobbers Canyon "pushed residential development elsewhere in downtown…and led to the renovation of more old buildings and the construction of new ones." Defending the loss of Jobbers Canyon, Shukert said, "Even in the worst-case scenario, it created a very important open space that people will continue to enjoy, and that adds value to the property."

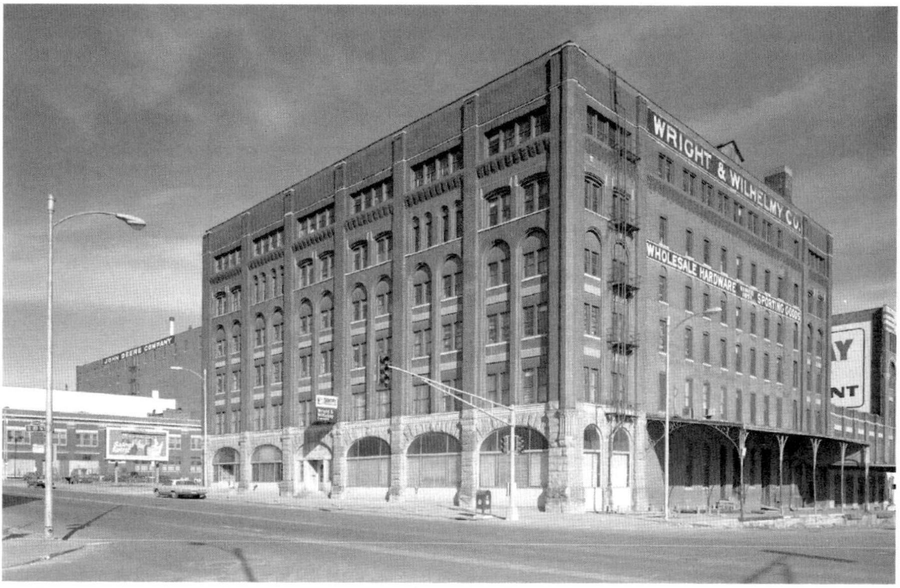

Wright & Wilhelmy Hardware Wholesalers. *Courtesy of City of Omaha, Landmarks Heritage Preservation Commission, Meyer Collection.*

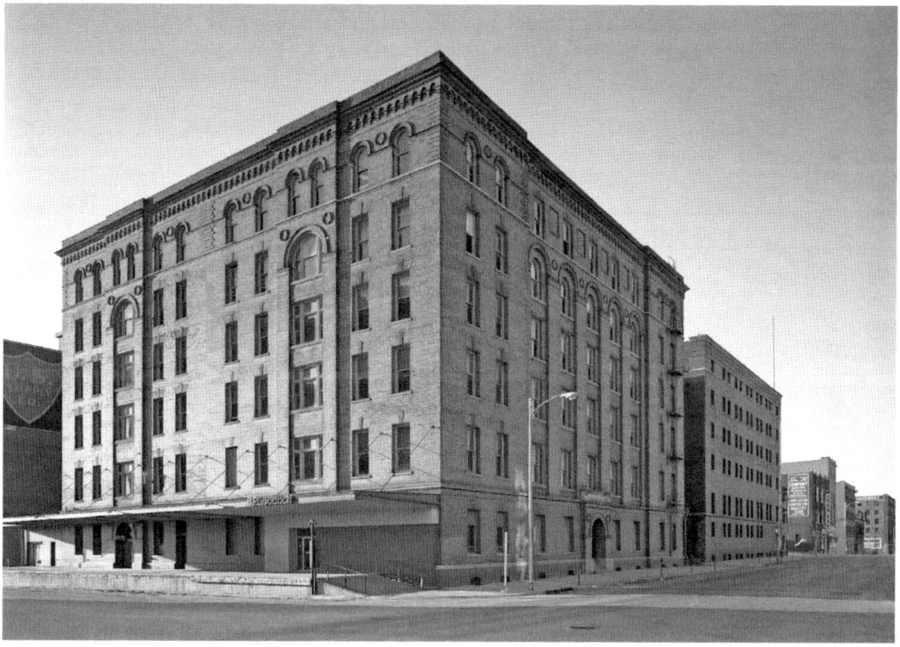

Jobbers Canyon was filled with six- to eight-story warehouse buildings. *Courtesy of City of Omaha, Landmarks Heritage Preservation Commission, Meyer Collection.*

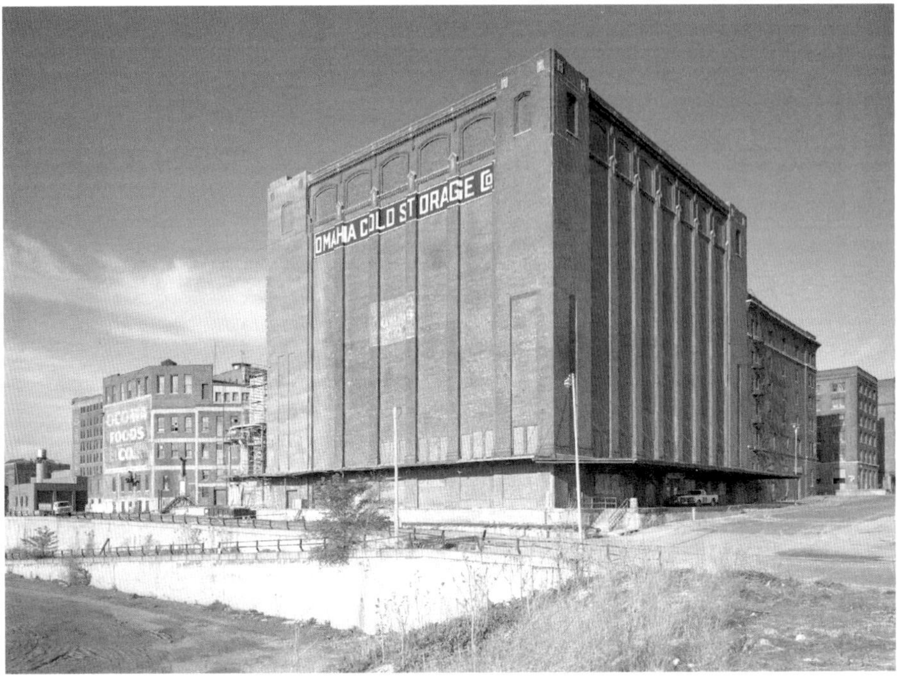

Very visible along the waterfront was the Omaha Cold Storage Building. *Courtesy of City of Omaha, Landmarks Heritage Preservation Commission, Meyer Collection.*

One piece of Jobbers Canyon does still survive. Included in the original historic district designation, but just outside the core six-block area, one building of the old Nash Block escaped demolition. The Nash Block, designed by Thomas Kimball, was a two-building complex built between 1905 and 1907. Catherine Nash, a widow and major real estate investor, financed construction of the buildings for the M.E. Smith Company, a dry goods firm. The twin buildings were connected over a rail alley. The complex (which eventually included a third building) served the M.E. Smith Company until the late 1930s. From the late 1930s until 1979, McKesson & Robbins, a pharmaceutical wholesaler, occupied the complex, primarily the south building; Pendleton Woolen Mills occupied the north building from the mid-1950s until 1979, when it sold its facility to the City of Omaha. In 1980, the city demolished the north building and the third building as part of the Central Park Mall project. In 1985, the Schneider Group of Ann Arbor, Michigan, bought the south building, also known as the McKesson-Robbins Building, which had been placed as an individual building in the

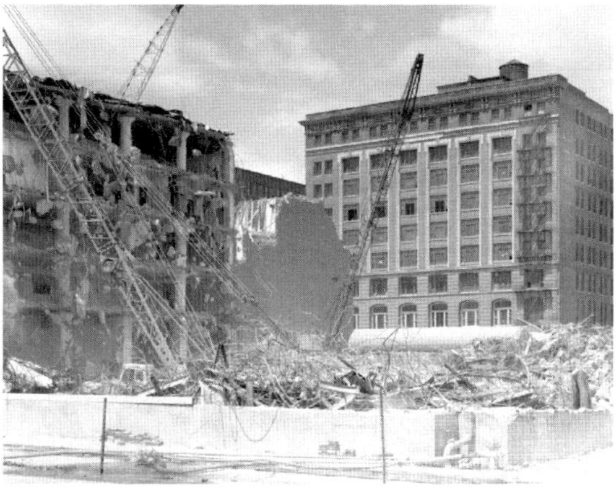

Demolition underway in Jobbers Canyon. *Courtesy of City of Omaha, Landmarks Heritage Preservation Commission, Meyer Collection.*

National Register in 1981. The Schneider group transformed the building into an apartment and office complex known as the Greenhouse that opened in 1987.[121] Marty Shukert, in 2015 an architect in private practice, had his office in the old McKesson-Robbins Building.[122]

Creative destruction of the Jobbers Canyon area was not limited to the late twentieth century. As Jobbers Canyon gave way to the ConAgra complex, a couple of newspaper articles reminded Omahans that earlier landmarks had also given way to allow for the creation of the warehouse district. Catherine Nash built the original two M.E. Smith Buildings at a site on which once stood a nineteenth-century log cabin that served as Nebraska's first territorial capitol. When, in 1922, a third building was added to the complex, its construction required the demolition of what had been the Herndon House Hotel. The Herndon House, built in 1858, was Omaha's first hotel. It was named in honor of U.S. Navy lieutenant William Lewis Herndon, who died commanding a mail ship lost in a storm off Panama in 1857. Two years after his death, his daughter, Ellen, married Chester A. Arthur. She died in 1880, before Arthur became the twenty-first president of the United States, serving from 1881 to 1885. The Herndon House underwent several changes in ownership until, in 1870, the Union Pacific leased the property as its headquarters. In 1875, the Union Pacific purchased the building and over the years both renovated and expanded the structure. The railroad company left the building in 1911, using it for storage until it was demolished in 1922.[123]

And on October 14, 1907, the local newspaper reported on the last services at St. Philomena's Cathedral in downtown Omaha. Built in 1868, St. Philomena's served as the cathedral church of the Omaha diocese until

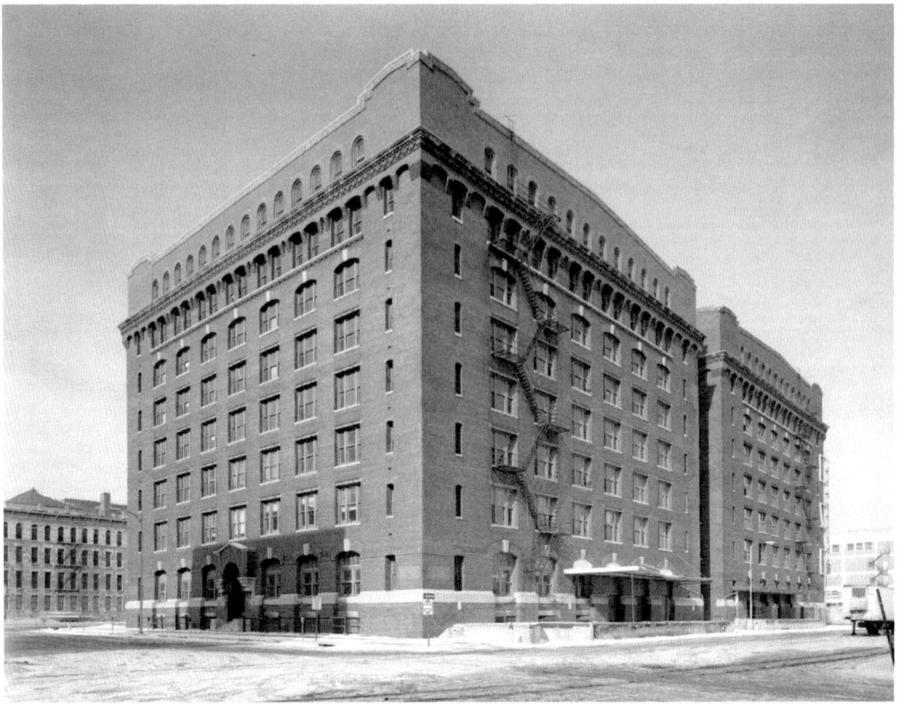

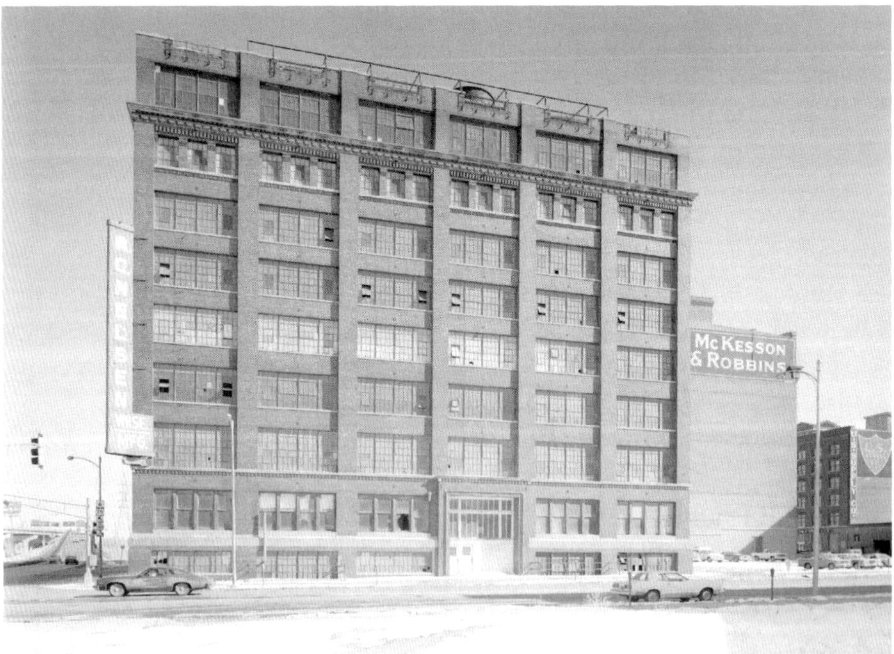
McKesson
& Robbins

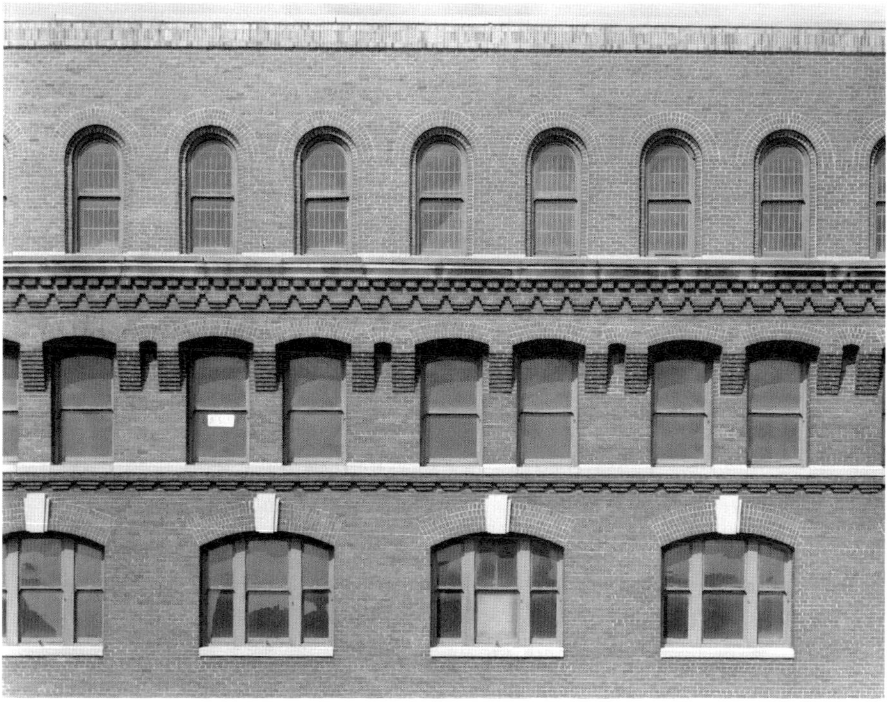

Above: Architectural detail on the south building. *Library of Congress, Prints & Photographs Division, HABS, HABS NE-36.*

Opposite, top: This view is looking north; the south building (the Greenhouse) still exists, while the north building was demolished to make way for the Gene Leahy Mall. *Library of Congress, Prints & Photographs Division, HABS, HABS NE-36.*

Opposite, bottom: The building housing A.C. Nelson was the third building in the complex; you can see the McKesson & Robbins sign on the south building; this building was also demolished to make way for the Gene Leahy Mall. *Library of Congress, Prints & Photographs Division, HABS, HABS NE-35.*

the early twentieth century, when the diocese began construction on a new cathedral, St. Cecilia's. Just as many would later lament the demolition of Jobbers Canyon, many mourned the loss of what was once described "as one of the most magnificent buildings in Omaha." The reporter stated, "Bathed in the tears of hundreds of old men and old women who had worshipped, wedded and buried their dead within its old brick walls, the old St. Philomena Cathedral held its last public service yesterday morning." (Note how both the worshipers and church were all repeatedly described as old.) St. Philomena, at Ninth and Howard, stood in the way of the expanding warehouse district. The John Deere Company built a warehouse on the site of the former cathedral in 1908. In 1988, the local newspaper compared the loss of St. Philomena's to the loss of Jobbers Canyon. "Now, as history repeats itself, a new generation of development is being made ready in the same area. Some of the structures that crowded out the old cathedral are themselves being targeted for removal. Thus continues the story of growth, change and renewal in the place once known as the neighborhood of St. Philomena's in old Omaha City—a place that is known more widely today by a different name: Jobbers Canyon." The newspaper article suggested that such creative destruction was both inevitable and desired, as it also noted that the demolition of St. Philomena's "helped the city grow and provided downtown jobs."[124] The concept of creative destruction certainly helps describe at least part of the process behind the loss of both St. Philomena's and Jobbers Canyon. However, the choice to build a new cathedral to replace St. Philomena's certainly played a role as well. And as for Jobbers Canyon, contingency (i.e., Enron's departure from the city and ConAgra's threat to leave Omaha unless given the riverfront site) and choice both played significant roles in determining its fate.

Omaha Stockyards and Packinghouse District

Omaha's stockyards dated to 1883. The Union Stockyards Company, founded by a Wyoming cattleman and six prominent Omaha businessmen, purchased two hundred acres of land south of Omaha in what became the separate city of South Omaha (incorporated 1886; annexed to Omaha in 1915). Construction began in April 1884, and the yards opened for business on August 25, 1884. At first, the yards served as an intermediate point for livestock on their way to Chicago. Organizers realized that the stockyards needed a local market for the cattle, hogs and sheep. Consequently, Alexander Swan, the Wyoming cattleman, began recruiting meatpackers to open shop in South Omaha. In short order, several meatpacking firms opened operations near the stockyards, including Armour, Cudahy and Swift. Along with Nelson Morris & Company, they were the first "Big Four" of Omaha's meatpacking industry. (Wilson replaced Morris in the 1930s.) The stockyards and packinghouses created thousands of jobs. South Omaha grew so rapidly that it became known as the "Magic City."[125]

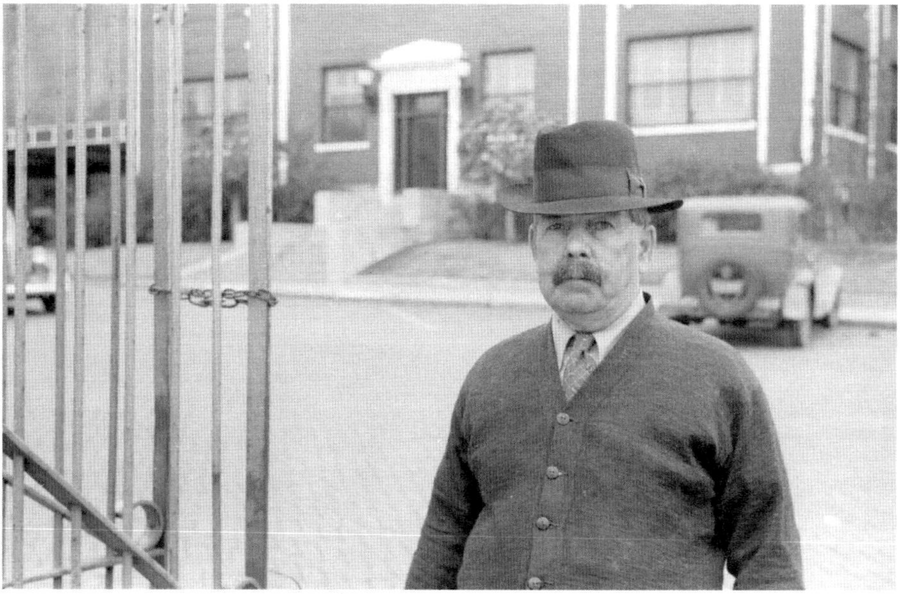

Thousands worked at the stockyards and packing plants. *Library of Congress, Prints & Photographs Division, FSA/OWI Collection, LC-DIG-fsa-8a03810.*

Omaha's stockyards thrived throughout the first half of the twentieth century. In 1956, they surpassed Chicago as the largest in the world. They would hold that title until 1973. Changes, though, were in the wind. The meat industry—aided by interstate highways and truck transportation—decentralized. Feedlots and newly automated packing plants in rural areas replaced the large centralized operations based on rail transportation. As long as the "Big Four" meatpackers retained operations in Omaha, however, the stockyards remained a vital source of cattle, hogs and sheep. The beginning of the end for both the stockyards and the meatpacking industry in Omaha began in the late 1960s.

Even as Omaha still identified itself as a center of the meatpacking industry, one by one the "Big Four" shut down their local plants. The first to go was Cudahy. Michael Cudahy left school at age fourteen to work in a Milwaukee meatpacking plant. He rose in the ranks to serve as a manager in Armour's plant in Chicago. In 1886, he and his brother Edward, with financing from Armour, opened the Cudahy-Armour plant in Omaha. A few years later, the Cudahys bought out Armour's interest. For many years, the Cudahy plant was the city's largest, and the company's headquarters remained in the city until 1911, when it moved to Chicago. When the

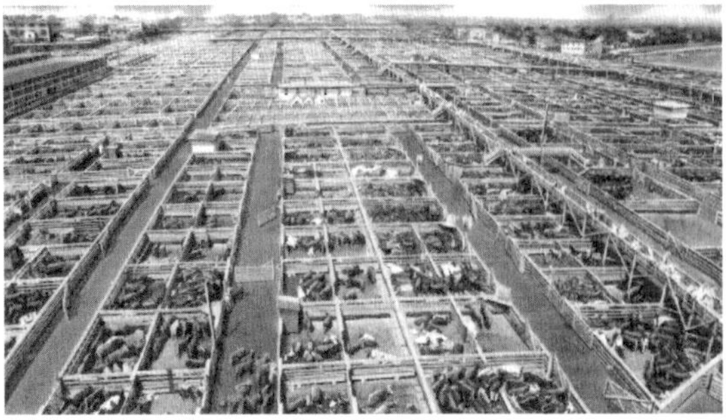

The stockyards in Omaha were also a tourist attraction. "Union Stock Yard Pens, Omaha, Nebraska." Card, 1930. *Digital Commonwealth, ark.digitalcommonwealth.org/ark:/50959/xs55mk13d (accessed August 19, 2016).*

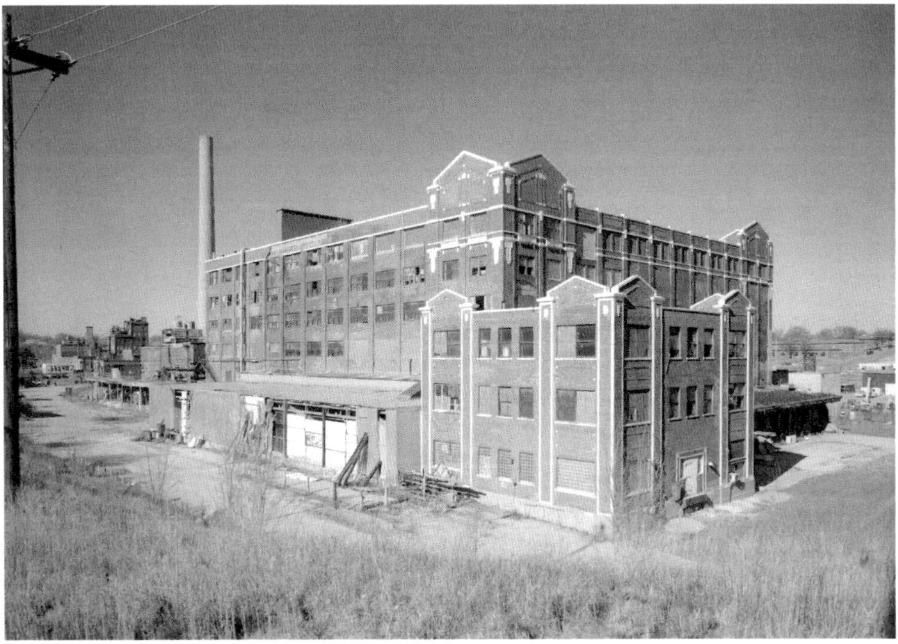

The Skinner Meatpacking plant shortly before its demolition. *Library of Congress, Prints & Photographs Division, HAER, HAER NE-12.*

company ended its Omaha operations in 1967, the Cudahy plant was actually one of the newest in the city. The company built the new facility in 1961 at a cost of $4.6 million. Industry restructuring and labor disputes in the 1960s contributed to the closure. The company experienced major labor battles with its Omaha workforce in 1962, 1963 and 1965. The 1965 battle was the largest, with the workers claiming the company was locking them out and the company claiming that the workers were on strike. The struggle lasted for four months, with the mayor of Omaha eventually

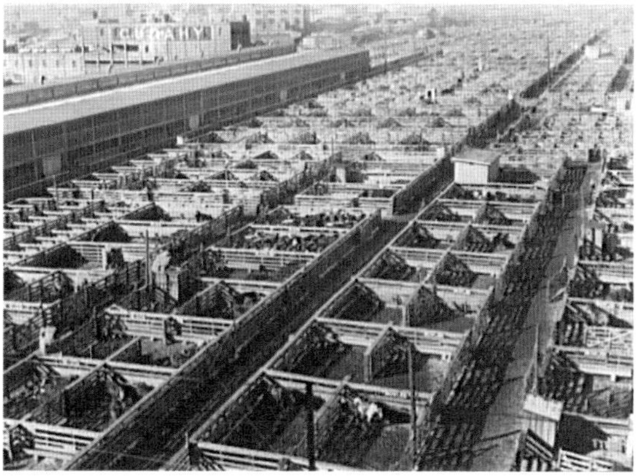

View of the stockyards; you can see the Cudahy plant in the background. *Library of Congress, Prints & Photographs Division, FSA/OWI Collection, LC-USF34-008880-D.*

stepping in to help settle the dispute. The plant only partially reopened after the strike. Following the 1965 dispute, the company stopped its hog slaughter operations. The company had already ended its sheep slaughter operations in the early 1960s.Only the cattle operations remained, and that was what closed in 1967. In the end, its small dry meat (sausage) and pharmaceutical operations were all that remained.[126]

The next to go was Armour. The company had actually given the city some hope when it purchased the former Cudahy plant in 1967. Within a year, however, in June 1968, the company announced it was closing its historic plant. The former Cudahy facility remained in operation for a short time, but it closed a few months later. The Armour closing was a much bigger blow to the South Omaha area than had been Cudahy's. Armour was the largest employer in the meatpacking sector in the city. The loss of the 2,200 jobs at the plant represented the largest job loss in the history of the industry in the city. Unlike the Cudahy plant, the Armour facility was one of the oldest in the city. The plant site was sold to a couple local salvage firms and was demolished almost immediately.[127] Just a few months after Armour closed, Swift announced it, too, would close its Omaha plant. The Swift plant, originally built in 1887, employed 1,600.[128] Wilson hung on for a few more years but closed its plant in 1976.[129]

The job losses were significant. Many of the employees, though, were older and eligible for pensions. The newspaper reported that most of the younger workers either moved to work for plants in other cities or managed to find jobs elsewhere in the city, though perhaps not at the same pay level they enjoyed at the plant. Those factors helped soften the blow to the workers somewhat but not completely. The story was largely the same after every plant closure. The workers were sad but not surprised. B.J. Ladd, who

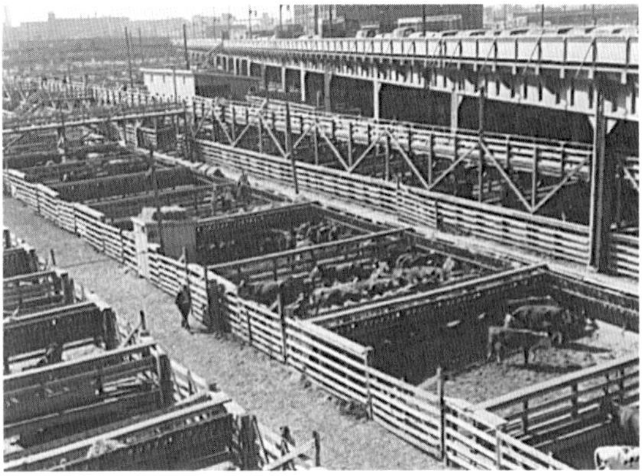

A view of the cattle pens, with cattle; you can get a sense of the scale from the person walking through the pens. *Library of Congress, Prints & Photographs Division, FSA/OWI Collection, LC-USF34-059877-D.*

worked at the Armour plant, noted, "I just sort of accept it. They are going to close and there is nothing I can do about it." He did not yet know what he was going to do and feared he might have to take two jobs to make the $3.18 per hour he earned as a pork trimmer. Clemens Kosiba, who worked for Armour for twenty years, had already decided to open a bar in a building he owned near Forty-Ninth and L. He worried, though, that the closing would hurt business.[130] A local union leader simply remarked after the Swift closing: "This is a sad day for Swift employees."[131]

Further, nothing could make up for the loss of the community and culture that had grown up around the plants. Lonny Liss, who owned a café and bar in the packinghouse district, said of the Armour closing, "All the merchants on Q Street are concerned about the closing. Some businesses have already closed. Somebody has got to build another plant there. But until they do, it's going to be rough." He had only a few workers in his place at the time of the interview. He told the reporter that the place "used to be jammed at this time. It's the lunch hour. But about a month ago the guys started cutting their spending and I had to close the kitchen."[132]

The Swift, Armour and Cudahy plants soon disappeared from the landscape. They were replaced by the South Omaha Industrial Park. In 1976, UPS opened a district distribution center on the site of the Swift plant. It employed hundreds. Metropolitan Technical Community College purchased twelve acres—with plans to purchase more—to build a new South Omaha campus.[133]

The Wilson plant, however, remained at Thirtieth and Y for several decades. A company called Mid-West Animal Products bought it shortly after the closure. Ten years later, Otis Glebe, a notorious Omaha slum landlord, bought the property. While he called the building "spectacular and

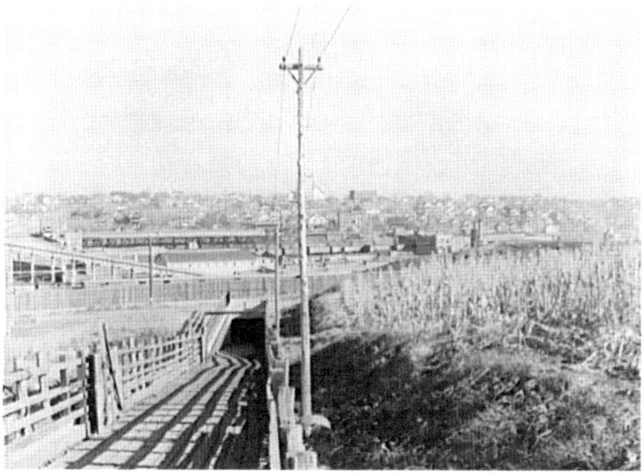

The tunnel between the stockyards and the packinghouses. *Library of Congress, Prints & Photographs Division, FSA/OWI Collection, LC-USF34-008821-D.*

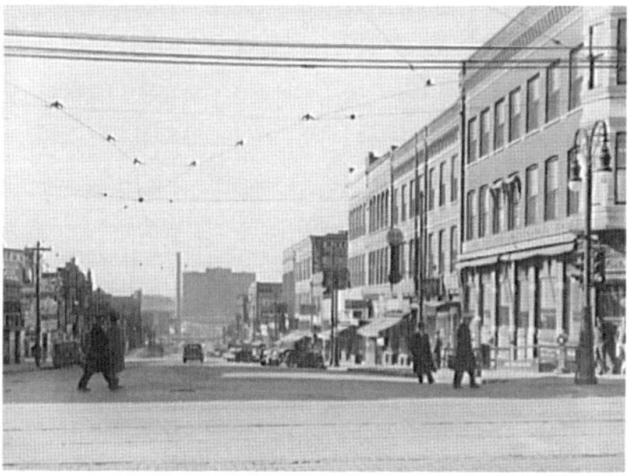

Downtown South Omaha with the stockyards (Livestock Exchange Building) in the background. *Library of Congress, Prints & Photographs Division, FSA/OWI Collection, LC-USF34-008960-D.*

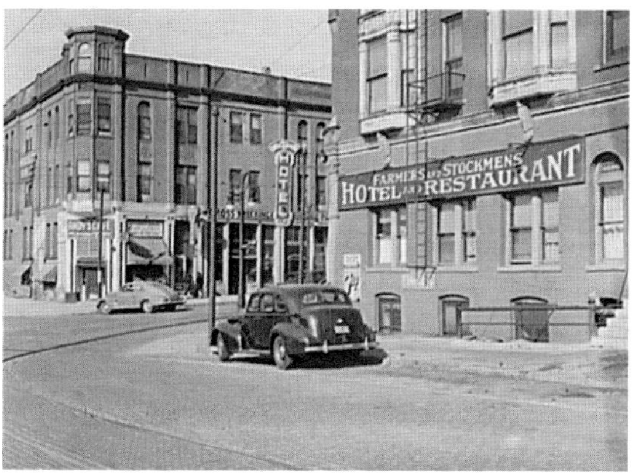

A hotel and restaurant serving the people working in the stockyards and packing plants. *Library of Congress, Prints & Photographs Division, FSA/OWI Collection, LC-USF34-090076-D.*

irreplaceable" and talked of rehabilitating it, he primarily used the plant to store what the neighbors and the city considered junk, including derelict cars, trucks, trailers and automobile parts. Glebe and his brother also lived in the facility, even after the city condemned the structure in 1992. After a protracted legal battle, the city gained title in 2001. Before the building's final demolition in 2002, a project manager for the demolition company noted "his crews [had] hauled out 550 to 600 semitrailer loads of refuse from the building and still [had] another 50 or so to go before the remainder of the building [could] be demolished in January." Most of the neighbors—who fought for years to have the city condemn and demolish the building—considered it an eyesore and nuisance. A former employee, Lee Valencia, said, "I made a lot of good money here. But it's served its time." After the demolition, another former employee, Elsia Hobbs, who lived near the plant for more than three decades, declared, "It was good when it served the community, but I'm glad it is gone." The site remained vacant for several years following the demolition. An effort to build a veterans' home collapsed after the state chose a site in Bellevue. Finally, the Salvation Army opened a Kroc Center on the site in 2009.[134]

Despite the loss of the large packing plants, the Omaha Stockyards remained in business—at least for a while. The stockyards continued in operations until 1999. However, over the years, the stockyards themselves shrank from covering over two hundred acres to about fifty and changed hands several times. In 1997, the City of Omaha announced a redevelopment plan for the area. Under the program, the "unsightly pens and run-down buildings" would "be replaced by small, light-manufacturing plants." Metropolitan Community College, which had already built a campus nearby, would expand. Neighbors had been complaining about the "smell and the

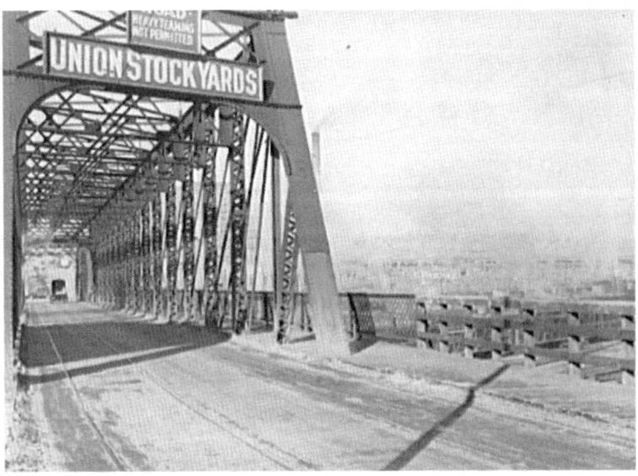

The entrance to the Omaha Stockyards. *Library of Congress, Prints & Photographs Division, FSA/OWI Collection, LC-USF34-008861-D.*

look of what remains of the industry that built South Omaha." They did not want the city to recruit new packinghouses to the area. Instead, they supported the expansion of the college and the preservation of the Livestock Exchange Building.[135]

In August 1999, people came from as far as three hundred miles away to attend an event in which they could purchase a piece of Omaha Stockyards history. Bette Votaw, for example, came from Wellfleet, Nebraska, and bought four drinking glasses with the Union Stockyards logo. Her father-in-law, Eli Votaw, had shipped cattle to the stockyards for more than fifty years. Others bought boxes of brass keys engraved with the initials USY (Union Stockyards) or a stack of unissued stock certificates. The sale happened a few weeks before the stockyards hosted the last livestock sale in the city in late October 1999—56 cows and bulls, 29 fatted steers and 650 hogs. Within a few days, the livestock market would open again, but in Red Oak, Iowa. Darrell Johnson had spent most of his life living and working around the stockyards. "I've been coming here since I was big enough to get out of the house….I guess it ended for me when I retired, but now this is the final ending of it in Omaha. It's like a family….I'm here today because after being around [it] all your life, you want to be here on the last day." Jim Nichol from Blair, who sold cattle at the yards from 1955 until 1999, stated, "It's been a good place for a lot of years. I never thought the place would close. I can remember when you had to wait at the chutes for a half hour to unload. But those days are gone."[136]

As noted previously, one part of the old stockyards and packinghouse district was preserved: the Livestock Exchange Building. The current building is the fourth to serve as the home of Omaha's livestock exchange. When the stockyards first opened, a nearby farmhouse provided the office space. Very quickly, however, operations outgrew the modest structure, and a new three-story building was built on O Street, but within a year, a third building was constructed nearby. In 1924, however, as Omaha housed the largest sheep market in the world and the second-largest livestock market in the country, the Omaha Livestock Exchange broke ground on a new headquarters. Local architect George Prinz designed the eleven-story structure. The H-shaped building, constructed by Peter Kiewit and Sons, "was built to be as fireproof as possible with a steel frame encased in concrete, reinforced concrete floors and brick curtain walls." The building, opened in 1926, soon became an important center not just of the livestock industry in Omaha but for the community generally. At its height in the 1950s, up to one thousand people would visit the building every day. Most would come

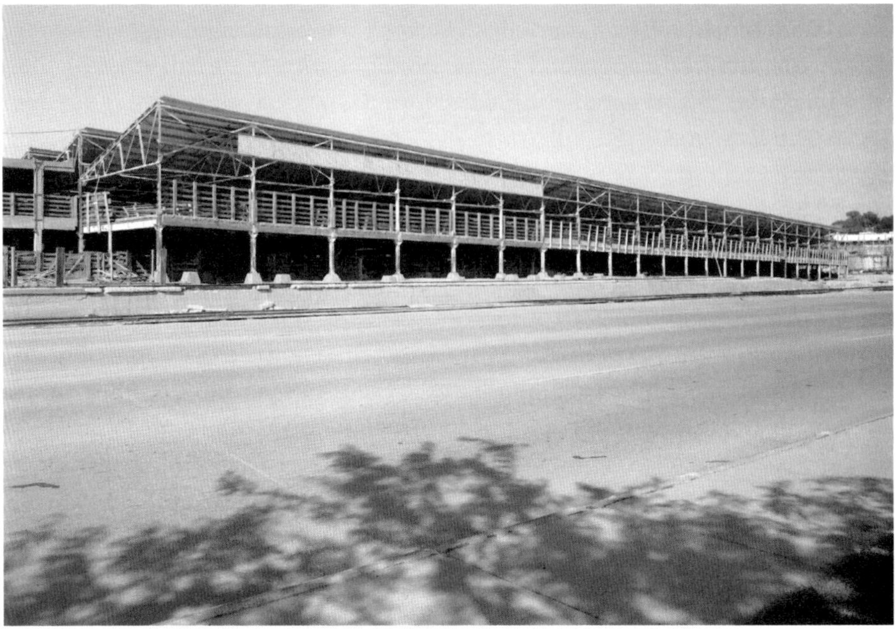

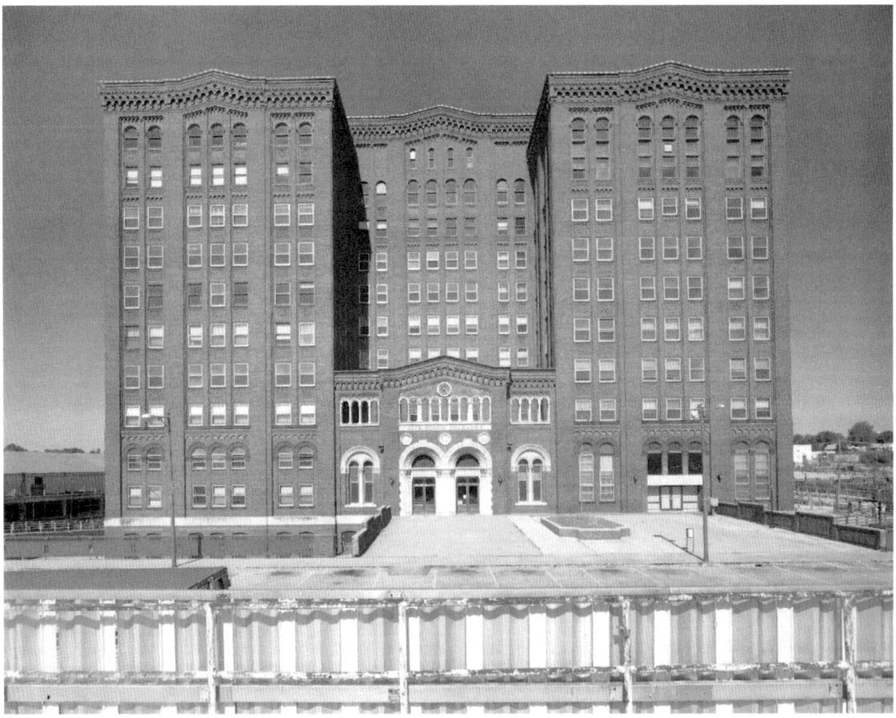

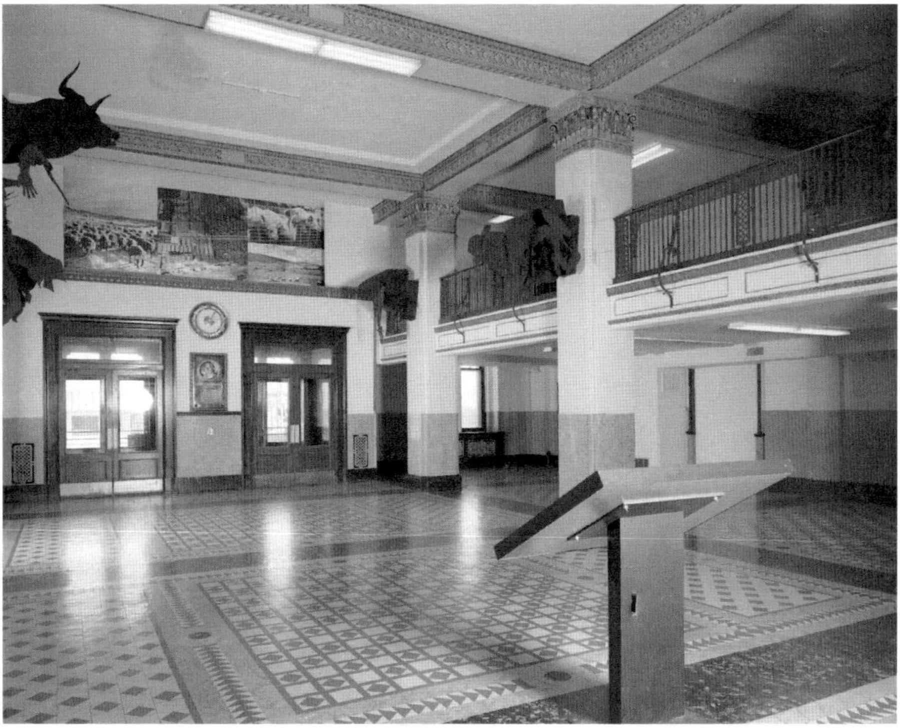

Above: Interior of the Livestock Exchange Building. *Library of Congress, Prints & Photographs Division, HAER, HAER NE-10-A-11.*

Opposite, top: Hog pens. *Library of Congress, Prints & Photographs Division, HAER, HAER NE-10-N.*

Opposite, bottom: The Livestock Exchange Building is still a major landmark in South Omaha. *Library of Congress, Prints & Photographs Division, HAER, HAER NE-10-A-1.*

on stockyard business, but others would come to shop for clothing, visit a doctor, get a haircut or do their banking. Most of the building's eleven stories housed offices of commission agents. The top two floors "on each leg of the building are ballrooms with massive windows."[137] The building currently houses apartments, the ballrooms (for weddings and special events) and other community space.

Creative destruction. As an older Omaha gave way to a new Omaha, one could wish that in places someone would have found a way to be more creative and less destructive. Omaha lost the Hotel Fontenelle at just the

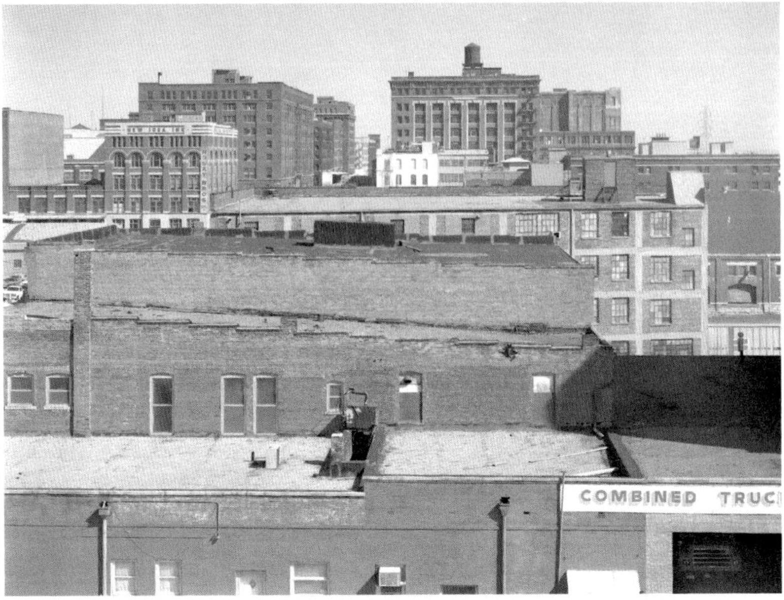

When Charles Harper of ConAgra viewed Jobbers Canyon, all he saw were old brick buildings. *Courtesy of City of Omaha, Landmarks Heritage Preservation Commission, Meyer Collection.*

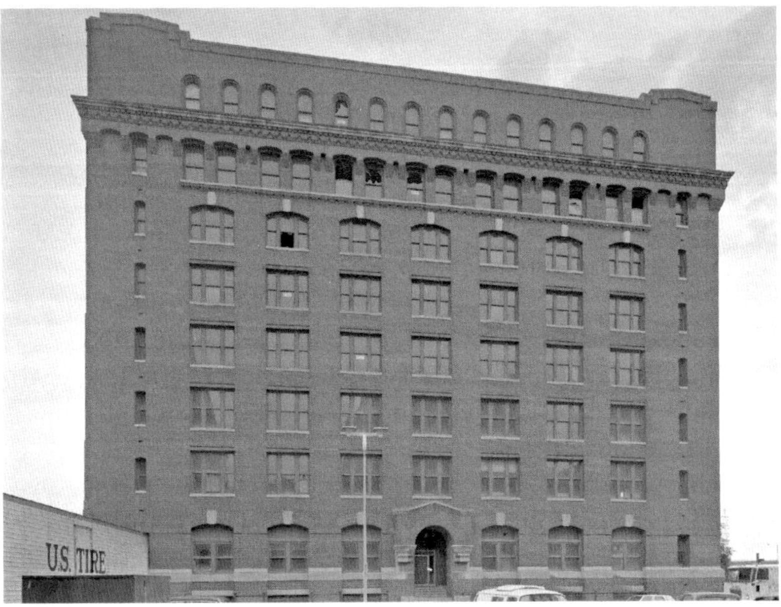

Preservationists, on the other hand, saw tremendous potential for reuse and redevelopment. *Courtesy of City of Omaha, Landmarks Heritage Preservation Commission, Meyer Collection.*

time that developers in other cities were rediscovering grand old hotels and refurbishing them for a new generation. Many cities had downtown athletic clubs. Many of those clubs closed. Yet in many cities, those club buildings survive as unique forms of downtown housing. And looking at the photographs of many of the buildings in Jobbers Canyon, one cannot help but wonder why ConAgra, Charles Harper and Omaha's civic leaders couldn't have been more creative when looking at what Harper called those "big, ugly red brick buildings"[138] and couldn't have found a way to house the company's new headquarters and create an authentic, multiuse riverfront district. The study of history is focused on change over time. Preserving significant parts of the past is important, though, to understanding that change. But even when the actual artifacts—the amusement parks, the racetracks, the warehouse districts, the office buildings—are gone, we can still learn something when we remind ourselves when and where and why they once existed and when and where and why they were lost.

CHAPTER 4

GONE, BUT PERHAPS HAPPILY FORGOTTEN

THE ASARCO LEAD REFINERY

It seldom received more than a passing note in histories of the city. It was, however, closely associated with one of the most storied families in Omaha history: the Nash family. Occasionally, the chamber of commerce would boast of it, as it was the largest of its kind in the world at one point. Of it, Hal Daub, former mayor of Omaha, noted, "Sometimes you have to tear down old stuff because you can't see past the ugliness of what's there in order to envision what could be there."[139] It was the ASARCO Lead Refinery located along the banks of the Missouri River just north of the ConAgra headquarters and Heartland of America Park (formerly Jobbers Canyon). And it gave way to the riverfront development that further transformed the eastern part of downtown Omaha in the late 1990s and early 2000s. Its legacy of pollution, however, made it one Omaha landmark whose passing was noted but not widely mourned.

In 1870, eight Omaha businessmen—C.H. Downs, William H. Pier, John A. Horbach, W.W. Lowe, A.L. King, Leopold Balbach, C.W. Mead and C.B. Rustin—formed the Omaha Smelting Company. They built the company's first buildings along the riverfront on Douglas Street. Rustin soon lured a newcomer to the city—Edward Watrous Nash—to work for the company. Nash, born in 1846, had come to Omaha with his bride, Catherine Barbeau Nash, in 1868. Nash rose to become secretary and then treasurer of the new concern. He reinvested most of his earnings in the company, and within a few years, he controlled it. He also invested in mining, banks, real estate and street railway companies. In 1882, Omaha Smelting merged with the Grant

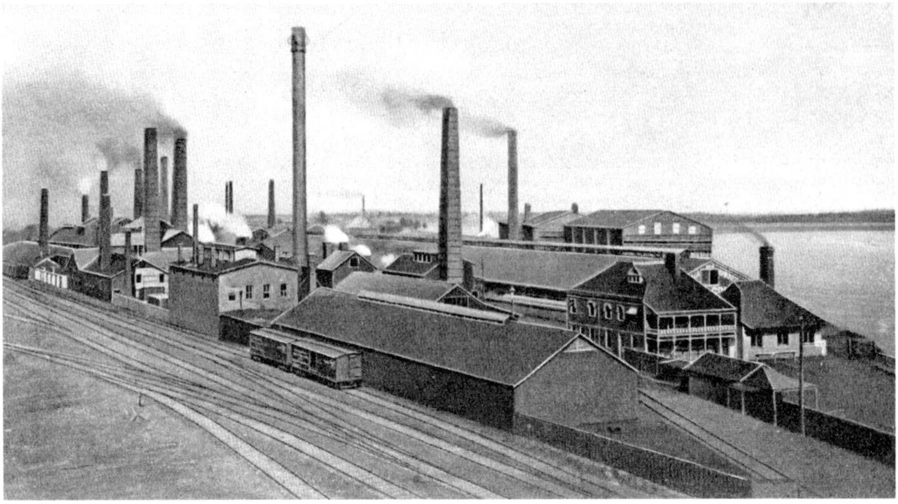

Omaha's connection to the lead industry began with the establishment of the Grant Smelting and Refining Company. *Courtesy of the Omaha Public Library Collection.*

Smelting Company of Denver. The wisdom of Nash's investment in lead became most apparent in 1899, when fifteen companies merged to form the American Smelting and Refining Company (later ASARCO). E.W. Nash was the new company's first president, a position he held until his death from a heart attack in 1905. An early history of Omaha described him as "a far-seeing and successful financier, a man of the highest integrity, and equipped with a vast fund of useful and varied information."[140] His widow, Catherine, also became an important investor in Omaha real estate, commissioning the construction of the complex of buildings known as the Nash Block for the M.E. Smith Company in 1905 and 1907. His brother Frederick A. Nash married a daughter of John Creighton, and their daughter, Emma Creighton Nash, served as the queen of AK-SAR-BEN in 1928.

In 1901, Daniel Guggenheim, the chairman of the American Smelting and Refining Company, came to Omaha on an inspection tour of the company's many production facilities. Much to the delight of Omaha boosters, Guggenheim declared, "It is the finest plant in the country and under exceptional management." He went on to note that while it was not the largest facility the company owned, it was the largest refinery not only in the United States but in the world "turning out more gold and other metals than any one plant." (The lead ore processed in Omaha contained "impurities" such as gold and silver that had to be removed.) He assured those at the plant that their future was secure, calling the facility "permanent" and saying that he expected that the facility would continue to grow.[141]

The local newspaper restated the plant's status as the largest refinery in the world in a 1925 article. After recounting the history of the company, the article then explained the products produced at the Omaha plant. The main products were two grades of lead—common and corroding—also noting that these products had an international reputation for quality. Corroding lead, the product with the highest purity, was used in the production of white lead paint. Common lead was used in the production of lead pipes and sheet lead. The plant also produced bismuth, used in the pharmaceutical industry. And, as noted previously, the refining process also resulted in the production of gold as well as silver, refined from the lead ore transferred to the Omaha plant from smelters located elsewhere in the United States.[142]

A few years later, the newspaper published an advertisement that celebrated the sixtieth anniversary of the establishment of lead refining in Omaha. By that date (October 27, 1929—just a few days after the start of the great stock market crash), however, the plant was only "one of the largest" refineries in the world but still the "world's largest producer of DESILVERED lead." In 1928, the refinery produced "170 thousand tons of lead, 18,500,000 ounces of silver and 108 thousand ounces of gold." The "thoroughly modern" facility covered thirteen acres and employed "several hundred workers."[143]

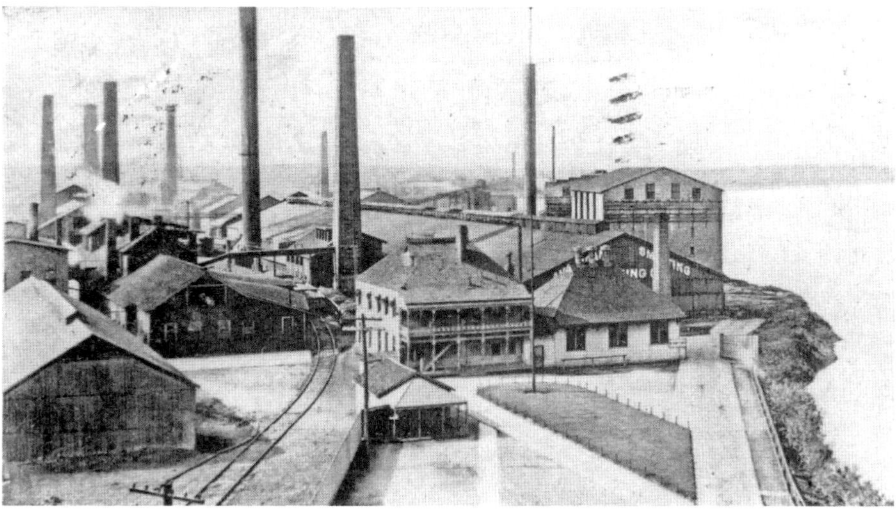

American Smelting and Refining was created in 1899 as a result of the merger of a number of lead smelting and refining companies, including Grant Smelting and Refining. *Courtesy of the Omaha Public Library Collection.*

And the newspaper once again highlighted the company in 1949—the fiftieth anniversary of the establishment of the American Smelting and Refining Company. The article in April 1949 declared that Omaha was now the home of "the largest lead refinery in the United States and the second largest in the world." This article went into more detail on the operations of the plant, describing the use of zinc in the process that separated gold and silver from the lead ore—called buttons—delivered to Omaha by rail.[144]

In fact, the refinery used a number of chemicals in the refining process. In addition to zinc, it used chlorine gas, calcium, caustic soda and sodium nitrate. It used these chemicals on the 181,855 tons of lead ore it refined in 1949 to produce 155,500 tons of refined lead. The article noted that most of the lead refined in Omaha was used in the production of storage batteries and cable covering. It was also used in the construction trade and as an additive in gasoline. "Lead is all around you in various forms," the article reminded readers. It made scant notice of the harm lead might cause, though it did note that smoke from the refineries' stacks was filtered "to prevent a harmful effect on the city." However, it was also noted that the filtering allowed the plant to "recover more of the valuable lead."[145]

The end for the refinery began with belated recognition of the environmental effects of its operations and, perhaps more importantly, a new set of ambitious plans to remake Omaha's riverfront. Talk of remaking the riverfront dated back to at least the 1960s, and plans periodically appeared over the several decades from the 1960s to the early 2000s. An initial riverfront scheme had resulted in the creation of the Central Park (now Eugene Leahy) Mall in the 1970s. The demolition of Jobbers Canyon and the creation of the ConAgra headquarters and Heartland of America Park marked another phase in the decades-long process. The most recent, and perhaps most dramatic, projects aimed at creating a new Omaha riverfront saw their inception between 1995 and 2003, during the terms of office of Mayor Hal Daub.

In 1995, Mayor Daub and the city council produced a new planning document focused on the eastern part of the downtown and its riverfront. That document had a number of important goals. The goal most important for the remaking of the downtown stated that the city must take action to enhance the downtown's role as the "image center" for the city.[146] Shortly thereafter, the leadership of several important Omaha businesses committed to major projects in the downtown. The Union Pacific Corporation, parent company of the Union Pacific Railroad, affirmed in 1997 that the railroad's headquarters would remain in the city. Then in 1999, the parent

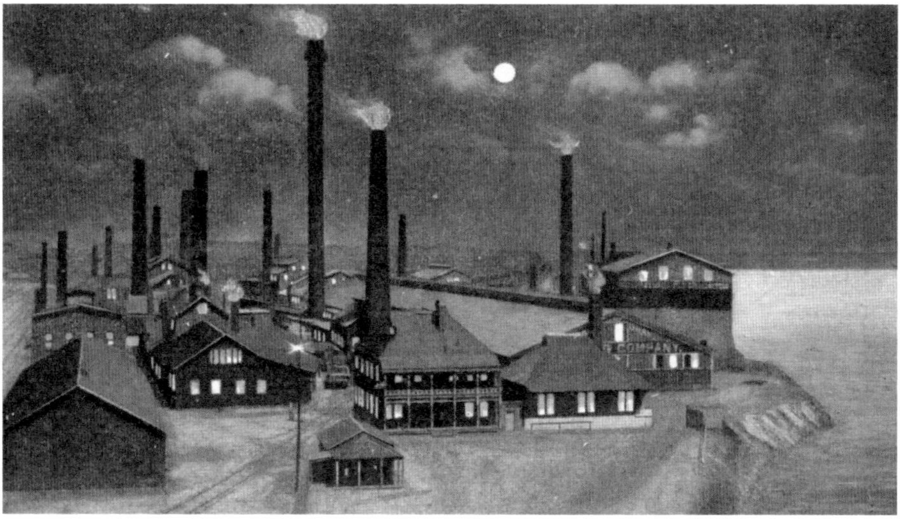

American Smelting and Refining merged with the Guggenheim interests in 1901. Edward Nash was a top executive. *Courtesy of the Omaha Public Library Collection.*

corporation announced that it would move its headquarters from Dallas, Texas, to Omaha. Though few jobs came with the move, it did result in the construction of a new headquarters building in downtown, completed in 2004.[147] Just a year before the Union Pacific made its announcement, First National Bank unveiled plans for a new headquarters building in September 1998. That building, completed in September 2002 (on the site of the old Medical Arts Building), soared forty stories over downtown (638 feet), making it the tallest building in the city.[148] And the local newspaper also committed to building its new production facility in the downtown.[149]

While all those projects gave great momentum to the new plans for Omaha's downtown and riverfront, the city had to do something about the ASARCO Lead Refinery operating on prime riverfront property. ASARCO had been under pressure to clean up its operations, particularly the release of lead into the atmosphere, for a number of years. In 1989, the company spent $6.7 million to install a new facility to improve the recovery of precious metals during the refining process and to reduce lead emissions. Immediately following the opening of the new facility, lead levels measured in the downtown area dropped, but in 1990, the U.S. Environmental Protection Agency reported that lead levels in the downtown area again exceeded federal standards. The blame was placed not on ASARCO but on demolition work around an old battery plant.[150] Nonetheless, the continued high lead levels resulted in renewed efforts by state and federal environmental agencies to reduce lead emissions.

The Nebraska Council of Environmental Quality issued a July 6, 1993 deadline for the company to cut lead emissions. As that deadline approached, the company requested a six-month extension. It argued that without the extension, it would have to close its Omaha operations, which employed 220. After a series of negotiations, the company agreed to spend $25.8 million on plant improvements and $1.9 million per year on operations to bring lead emissions down to healthy limits. The state then extended the deadline to January 6, 1997.[151] Meanwhile, reducing the air pollution the refinery produced was not the only problem the company faced, as in March 1994, two residents of Bellevue, Nebraska, a community just south of Omaha on the Missouri River, filed suit against ASARCO. Their concern was not air pollution but water pollution. This action came one day after the company filed suit against the Nebraska Council of Environmental Quality arguing that it had a valid permit to discharge wastes into the river. The following month, the U.S. Environmental Protection Agency filed suit to halt discharges into the river.[152] As the various suits made their way through the court system, a number of Omaha and Nebraska politicians began negotiations with the company. This time, their aim was to convince the company to move rather than improve.

About a year after the first lawsuits over water pollution were filed, Senator Bob Kerrey confirmed in March 1995 that he was leading negotiations between ASARCO and other local officials, including Governor Ben Nelson and newly elected mayor Hal Daub. Kerrey was interested in the creation of a park that would stretch along the Missouri River from the Heartland of America Park north along the river to near the airport. This park would be part of a larger complex of riverfront trails envisioned to stretch from the city of Tekamah to just south of Bellevue. Kerrey strongly suggested that ASARCO could spend the money it planned to use to meet environmental standards at its current location to instead fund a move to a new location.[153]

Negotiations continued through 1995 and into 1996. Finally, following a settlement of the federal lawsuit concerning discharge into the river, the city and ASARCO announced an agreement. Though the company suggested that it might build a new plant somewhere near the city, the agreement announced in April 1996 did not specify when or where. Instead, it simply stated that the company would close the refinery, demolish its buildings and perform an environmental cleanup so that by the end of 1998, the city would be presented with a twenty-three-acre grassy area that could be developed as a park. However, negotiations over some details of the plan, especially concerning cleanup and future liability, continued and delayed action. The company came to a final agreement with the state in September 1997; the city and the company signed a final deal on June 10, 1998. Operations of the refinery had ended in July 1997, and demolition began in August 1998. The company turned the property over to the city in 2000.[154]

Perhaps the only people upset with the closing were the 225 workers—most belonging to the Steelworkers Union—employed at the plant. Frank Truman, an employee and president of the union local, said, "We just felt like the city and the company and everyone else let us down." He noted that the average ASARCO employee had worked at the facility for twenty years. He estimated that the city would lose $22 million in wages and taxes. The union predicted that less than 10 percent of the workers would find employment at other ASARCO locations. Many signed up for early retirement. A company spokesman opined that workers "should be able to find jobs in Nebraska with its low unemployment rate."[155]

In July 2001, the City of Omaha officially decided on the name of the new park located on the refinery site. Initially, the city council approved the name Union Labor Plaza. However, after an election in May 2001, which witnessed the ousting of Mayor Daub and five city council members, the new mayor and council decided to review the earlier choice. After asking for public input, the council decided on Lewis and Clark Landing. Omaha's return to its riverfront involved not just massive physical transformations, such as the demolition of the lead refinery (and Jobbers Canyon before it), but an extensive reconceptualization of the downtown and riverfront. Omaha's historic downtown riverfront had been home to commerce, transportation and industry. Omaha's new downtown riverfront was home to open space, recreation, leisure and cultural amenities. "Union Labor Plaza" evoked the historic, somewhat gritty downtown riverfront. "Lewis and Clark Landing," on the other hand, hearkened back to a past that predated Omaha itself by a half century and evoked more pristine images of frontier, wilderness and adventure. Though the plaza eventually held a statue dedicated to Omaha's working people, the choice of the name suggested the degree to which Omaha's civic leadership had engaged in their own form of creative destruction—replacing the old image of Omaha and its downtown riverfront with the new.

Though gone, the lead refinery could not be forgotten. More than one hundred years of lead refining left its own unwelcome legacy in the city. In

2001, the EPA announced it was looking into declaring much of eastern Omaha a Superfund site due to "contaminated soils…contributing to high levels of lead in children's blood." City officials resisted the Superfund designation, fearing it would block economic development and lower property values. Race became an issue, as the area designated for Superfund status—east of Forty-Fifth Street (later expanded in places to Fifty-Second Street), L Street to Ames Avenue—included the city's minority neighborhoods. And although other sources of lead contamination were involved—lead paint, lead pipes—the EPA determined soil contamination as the major contributor to the high levels of lead found in children's blood. It also determined the lead refinery as the source of most of the soil contamination. Omaha received the Superfund designation in 2003, and at the time, it ranked as "one of the largest residential cleanups the government has undertaken." The EPA eventually tested soil at more than forty thousand properties in a twenty-seven-square-mile area. Remedial actions included "excavation of soil exhibiting lead concentrations greater than 400 ppm, replacement of contaminated soil with clean backfill, placement of sod, stabilization of lead-based paint to protect the remediated soil, testing of indoor dust, and public education and outreach to assist the public in recognizing other potential sources of lead contamination." The EPA completed its remedial work at the end of 2015, leaving the city responsible for future actions.[156]

CONCLUSION

SIX DEGREES OF LOST OMAHA AND THE AK-SAR-BEN BRIDGE

In 1929, Hungarian author Frigyes Karinthy published a collection of short stories based on the idea that the modern world was highly interconnected. A character in one of the stories theorized that any two individuals in the world could be linked together through no more than five other individual acquaintances. This theory was popularized in John Guare's play *Six Degrees of Separation* (later made into a movie starring Will Smith). Soon, many people began playing a variation of this in a game called "Six Degrees of Kevin Bacon"—the idea that any actor could be linked to Kevin Bacon though no more than five other actors who shared screen credits in a movie or commercial featuring Kevin Bacon. The modern world may not be as interconnected as the theory might suggest, but many of the parts of lost Omaha are linked.

For example, Jerry Malec, one of the brothers who developed Peony Park, died relatively young (age forty-six) in 1937. Nonetheless, he can be linked to many of the parts of lost Omaha beyond Peony Park. According to his obituary, Malec worked as the chief mechanic at the airmail field on the AK-SAR-BEN grounds. His connection to AK-SAR-BEN links him to Eugene Eppley (a king of AK-SAR-BEN) and, thus, the Fontenelle Hotel. It also links him to the Nash family—several of whom served as AK-SAR-BEN royalty (F.A. Nash, king in 1900; Louis Nash, king in 1922; Emma Creighton Nash, queen in 1928)—and thus to both Jobbers Canyon (the M.E. Smith Building and the Creighton Building, in particular) and the ASARCO lead refinery. His connection to the Hotel Fontenelle links him to Thomas Kimball, the architect, who also designed the Medical Arts Building. Additionally, his AK-SAR-BEN link connects him to Peter Kiewit (king in 1959) and the Stock Exchange Building, which Kiewit's family business built, and to George Brandeis (king in 1931), who helped found the Omaha Athletic Club. In fact, one could almost play the game as "Six Degrees of AK-SAR-BEN." For example, the architect George Prinz designed the Stock Exchange Building, and that links him to Peter Kiewit and AK-SAR-BEN and thus to all the other AK-SAR-BEN connections. John Latenser designed the M.E. Smith Building, and that links him to Catherine Nash, who was the mother of Louis Nash and, thus, linked to AK-SAR-BEN. AK-SAR-BEN even provides a link to the packinghouse district, as a Miss Jean Cudahy served as the queen of AK-SAR-BEN in 1908. This game suggests that many of Omaha's lost landmarks are linked to an interconnected group of individuals and families. In part those links—to prominent architects and families—are what made the places of lost Omaha landmarks in the first place.

AK-SAR-BEN can also be linked to an important transportation link in Omaha's history—another piece of lost Omaha, one that would have brought travelers into downtown Omaha near both Jobbers Canyon and the lead refinery and, should they continue their journey west, perhaps past Peony Park. That link was the AK-SAR-BEN Bridge. What became the AK-SAR-BEN Bridge began as the Douglas Street Bridge in 1888. It was the first highway bridge to cross the Missouri River between Council Bluffs and Omaha. The Omaha and Council Bluffs Street Railway Company built the structure to handle a very new invention: the electric streetcar. The bridge opened to streetcar traffic on October 30, 1888. Nebraska's governor, John M. Thayer, and Iowa's governor, William Larabee, both spoke at the event. The wives of the mayors of both Omaha and Council Bluffs officially christened the bridge by breaking bottles of wine against the rails at the center of the structure. Hundreds then marched in a parade that began at Twelfth and Farnam and included the Hibernian Band, the Edward Creighton Guards and the Custer Post of the Grand Army of the Republic.[157] Over time, the company expanded the width of the bridge, and eventually it carried not only streetcars but also automobiles and pedestrians. For all users except the streetcar company that owned it, it was a toll bridge. And as automobile traffic increased, so did the complaints of drivers over the tolls.

And that is where AK-SAR-BEN entered the story. In 1938, the civic organization purchased the bridge. The Knights promised that the bridge—which had apparently served as a major conduit for the transport of illicit

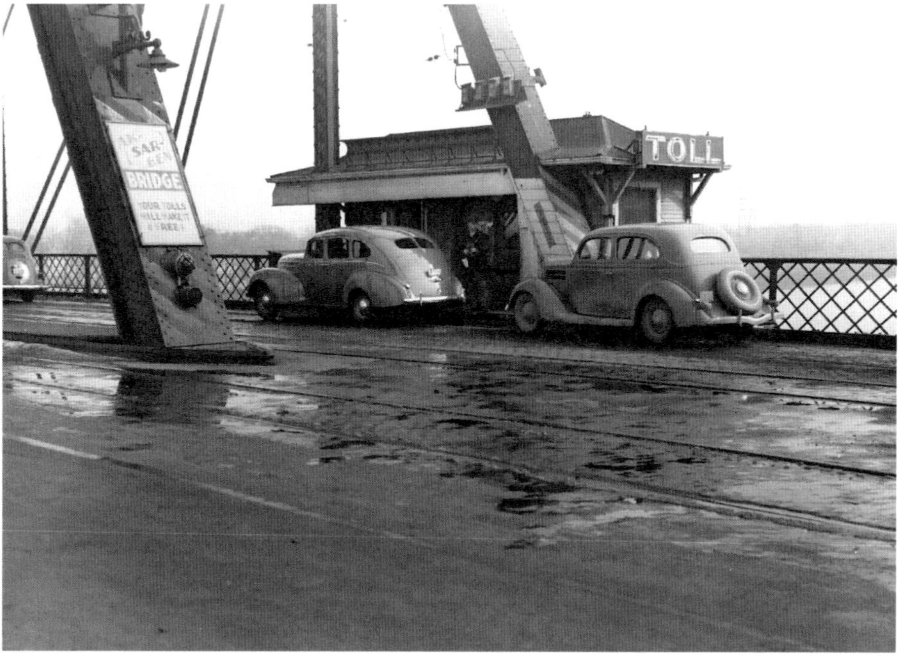

AK-SAR-BEN toll bridge. Tolls on the bridge proved very unpopular. AK-SAR-BEN purchased the bridge in 1938, promising to end the tolls, which did happen in 1947. *Library of Congress, Prints & Photographs Division, FSA/OWI Collection, LC-USF34- 008839-D [P&P].*

liquor during Prohibition—would become "free" once the tolls collected reimbursed the organization for the cost of its purchase. It took nine years, but on September 25 and 26, 1947, Omaha celebrated the end of tolls on the AK-SAR-BEN Bridge as well as the South Omaha Bridge. Travel by car into Omaha was finally free (at least until the construction of the Mormon Bridge in 1952). The local newspaper dubbed the event the "Dream of Decades." Once again, political and military figures played prominent roles in the civic celebration. Bands from North High School in Omaha and Thomas Jefferson High School in Council Bluffs also participated. A major parade wound its way through the streets of South Omaha while schools and businesses closed so that all could celebrate this event.[158]

The AK-SAR-BEN Bridge remained an important link between Omaha and Council Bluffs—as well as a part of a major east–west highway—until the 1960s. The advent of the interstate highway system spelled the end for the bridge. Interstate 480 connects Interstate 80 in Nebraska with Interstate 29 in Iowa. The construction of Interstate 480 not only led to the demolition of working-class and ethnic neighborhoods immediately west of the downtown but also resulted in the demolition of the AK-SAR-BEN Bridge. In 1966, a new Interstate 480 Bridge spanned the Missouri River between Council Bluffs and Omaha. With the completion of the new span, highway officials initially declared the closure of the AK-SAR-BEN Bridge on November 21, 1966. At 11:25 a.m. that day, Donna Hoden of Council Bluffs crossed the bridge on her way home from a shopping trip in Omaha. Once she crossed, workmen placed barricades on the roadway, officially closing the bridge. Miss Hoden, who was actually glad to see the old bridge close, lost her chance to go down in history as the last person to use the bridge when officials reopened it the following day due to traffic issues in Council Bluffs. The bridge remained opened to traffic until December 13, 1966, when a new ramp to the interstate bridge finally opened.[159]

The ultimate fate of the old bridge, however, was still in doubt. In 1964, the city councils of both Omaha and Council Bluffs agreed that the bridge would be demolished once the new interstate bridge was in place. By November 1966, however, the mayor of Council Bluffs favored preserving the bridge, and Omaha's city council created a committee to study the matter. The Omaha City Council held a public hearing on May 22, 1967, where several individuals spoke in favor of preserving the structure. City council member Robert Cunningham reported that the council had voted 6–1 to preserve the bridge. Cunningham noted that it was used by pedestrians. His comments were echoed by Council Bluffs council member Joseph Katelman, who said demolition of the bridge would amount to "discrimination" against walkers. Council member Betty Abbott spoke on behalf of "oldsters" she felt would be more comfortable using the old bridge rather than having to drive at interstate speeds. In the end, however, the meeting showed that there was a great deal of "moral" support for preservation but no funding.[160]

Demolition on the bridge began in 1967 and was complete in late 1968.[161] Why this attention to the AK-SAR-BEN Bridge even though its loss predated both the first and second waves of "creative destruction" in Omaha? First, it was another important local landmark associated with the civic organization that is now lost. But moreover, as noted previously, the AK-SAR-BEN Bridge not only carried streetcars (until the system shut down in 1955), automobiles and trucks, but it also provided pedestrians, including those on bicycles, a way to cross between Omaha and Council Bluffs. Pedestrians and cyclists were banned from the new interstate bridge. It was not until the riverfront development associated with the second wave of "creative destruction" that pedestrians and cyclists regained their ability to cross the Missouri River with the construction of the J. Robert Kerrey Pedestrian Bridge in 2008—forty years after the demolition of the AK-SAR-BEN Bridge and the emergence of a new (or renewed) sense that cities must be pedestrian friendly.

Though all these landmarks may indeed have significant points of shared connections, the meanings that they have for individual Omahans may vary considerably. As noted, for many Omahans Peony Park was a beloved amusement park and dance hall. For some, though, it was a site of racial tensions. Searching through the newspaper archives for items about the Hotel Fontenelle and the Omaha Athletic Club, the author was reminded of times when help wanted advertisements not only were divided between men and women but many advertisements also specified white or "colored." Further, workers and managers might have quite different memories of the packinghouses and the lead refinery. Some might object to any focus on the less celebratory aspects of the histories of these lost Omaha landmarks. However, just as well-behaved women seldom make history, one-dimensional stories seldom capture our imaginations. Wonderful events and happy memories are part of history, but so are conflicts, complexity and contradictions. Further, contested meanings provide opportunities for learning and dialogue. History is both rich and messy. The more we allow landmarks—both those lost and those preserved—to remind us of the messiness of our past, the richer we will be.

Further, the study of history is focused on change over time. Preserving significant parts of the past is important, though, to understanding that change. But even when the actual artifacts—the amusement parks, the racetracks, the warehouse districts, the office buildings—are gone, they still exist in memory, in photographs, in records and in the histories of the times in which they existed and that gave them their significance.

NOTES

Introduction

1. For an explanation of the concept and to see how it has been applied to change over time in Manhattan, see Max Page, *The Creative Destruction of Manhattan, 1900–1940* (Chicago: University of Chicago Press, 2001).
2. See "Population of the 100 Largest Cities and Other Urban Places in the United States, 1790–1990," www.census.gov/population/www/documentation/twps0027/twps0027.html.
3. Dorothy Devereaux Dustin, *Omaha & Douglas County: A Panoramic History* (Woodland Hills, CA: Windsor Publications, 1980), 68.
4. Janet R. Daly-Bednarek, *The Changing Image of the City: Planning for Downtown Omaha, 1945–1973* (Lincoln: University of Nebraska Press, 1992), 177–79.
5. Ibid.

Chapter 1

6. *Sunday World-Herald*, "Award Contract for New Medical Building," November 30, 1919.
7. *Sunday World-Herald*, "Work on New Medical Arts Building Begins," September 25, 1921; *World-Herald*, "Omaha at a Glance," August 24, 1922.

8. *Sunday World-Herald*, "Gaunt Steel Skelton Has Had Varied Career," August 24, 1924.
9. *Evening World-Herald*, "Kulp Will Finish Medical Arts as Office Building, "July 25, 1925.
10. *World-Herald*, "Valley Medical Men Assemble Here Today," September 15, 1926; *Evening World-Herald*, "Directory of Tenants, Medical Arts Building," December 22, 1926.
11. *Morning World-Herald*, "Body of Dr. Gifford Lies in State Today," November 29, 1929.
12. *Evening World-Herald*, "Largest Mortgage on Omaha Building," April 5, 1926; *World-Herald*, "Names Receiver as Medical Arts Interest Unpaid," August 9, 1930.
13. *Omaha World-Herald*, "Headed into History," April 19, 1998.
14. Ibid.
15. *Sunday World-Herald*, "Old Hall Returns to Action," June 8, 1980.
16. *Evening World-Herald*, "Eerie Cat Calls Pursue Elevator Up and Down Medical Arts Building," March 11, 1930.
17. *Evening World-Herald*, "4-Story Leap Kills Omahan," August 7, 1937; *Evening World-Herald*, "Omaha Woman, 67, Jumps to Death," October 27, 1938.
18. *Omaha World-Herald*, "Hotel-to-Tower Pedestrianway Almost a Maze," February 17, 1971.
19. *Sunday World-Herald*, "Plan Revealed for Cafeteria," May 14, 1950.
20. *Evening World-Herald*, "Items Designed for the Blind Fill Shelves of New Shop," February 17, 1961.
21. Janet R. Daly Bednarek, "Creating an 'Image Center': Reimagining Omaha's Downtown and Riverfront, 1986–2003," *Nebraska History* 90, no. 4 (Winter 2009): 202.
22. *Omaha World-Herald*, "50 Businesses to Get Moving Papers," November 8, 1996; *Omaha World-Herald*, "Implosion Is Expected to Be Downtown's Last," March 31, 1999; *Omaha World-Herald*, "Medical Arts Memories to Last Beyond the Rubble," April 2, 1999.
23. *Omaha World-Herald*, "After 73 Years Just a Pile of Rubble," April 3, 1999.
24. *Omaha World-Herald*, "Midlander of the Year," December 27, 2015.
25. Alfred Sorenson, *The Story of Omaha* (Omaha, NE: National Printing Company, 1923), 642–44.
26. *Morning World-Herald*, "Tribute of the Orator to the Work of Fontenelle," February 25, 1915.

27. *Lincoln Journal Star*, "Jim McKee: The Fontenelle Hotel, an Omaha Architectural Gem," October 20, 2013, journalstar.com/news/local/jim-mckee-the-fontenelle-hotel-an-omaha-architectural-gem/article_d3d7b3c3-18a4-5b79-b15e-7e165ce57ec6.html (accessed June 30, 2016).
28. *Sunday World-Herald*, "Manager of Hotel Fontenelle Is Dead," April 8, 1915.
29. *Evening World-Herald*, "Pershing Birthday Cake Weighs Just Half a Ton," September 11, 1918.
30. Harl Dahlstrom, *Eugene C. Eppley: His Life and Legacy* (Lincoln, NE: Johnsen Publishing Company, 1969), 1–12.
31. Ibid., 18–19.
32. Ibid., 19.
33. *Evening World-Herald*, "Barbara's Kindness Just Opened 'Heaven' for Adoring Omaha Candy Girl," April 29, 1939.
34. Dahlstrom, *Eugene C. Eppley*, 25–26.
35. Ibid., 20.
36. *Omaha World-Herald*, "70 Years Later, Vets Back to Fulfill Wartime Vow," August 31, 2014.
37. Dahlstrom, *Eugene C. Eppley*, 29–30.
38. *Sunday World-Herald*, "Fontenelle Hotel Employees Conducting a Silent Wake," February 28, 1971.
39. *Omaha World-Herald*, "Permanents Find New Homes," March 1, 1971.
40. *Sunday World-Herald*, "Once Grand Hotel Sits Dark, Silent and Alone," June 17, 1973.
41. *Omaha World-Herald*, "Three Times Fontenelle Hotel Made News on Feb. 28," March 1, 1977.
42. *Sunday World-Herald*, "'Majestic' Fontenelle Dream Is Dusted Off," November 4, 1979.
43. See Robert D. Putnam, *Bowling Along: The Collapse and Revival of American Community* (New York: Simon & Schuster, 2000).
44. *Sunday World-Herald*, "Sixty One Who Would Live in Athletic Club," April 9, 1916.
45. *Sunday World-Herald*, "View of Omaha Athletic Club from Architect's Picture," March 18, 1917.
46. *Sunday World-Herald*, "Omaha Athletic Club to Open Next Month," October 13, 1918.
47. *Sunday World-Herald*, "Athletic Club to Open Thursday Eve," December 8, 1918.

48. *Evening World-Herald*, "Athletic Club Opening Has Been Postponed," December 11, 1918.
49. *Evening World-Herald*, "Informal Opening in Place of Formal One," December 14, 1918.
50. *Sunday World-Herald*, "Enjoying the Silent Room at the Omaha Athletic Club," December 29, 1918.
51. *Sunday World-Herald*, "Athletic Club Begins Cash Basis March 1," February 26, 1933.
52. *Evening World-Herald*, "Receiver Is Named for Athletic Club," March 2, 1933; *World-Herald*, "O.A.C. Must Get 350 Members or Close," March 12, 1933; *Evening World-Herald*, "Creditors Take Over Athletic Club Assets," March 20, 1933.
53. *Evening World-Herald*, "Sees Bright Prospect Club Reorganization," September 10, 1936; *Sunday World-Herald*, "650 at Athletic Club Reopening," December 20, 1936.
54. *Evening World-Herald*, "Slot Machine 'Artists' Freed; Leave City," September 26, 1942.
55. *Morning World-Herald*, "Permit Slots in Private Clubs," April 11, 1942.
56. *Omaha World-Herald*, "Faded Glory, Athletic Club to Face the Wrecking Ball," January 6, 1992.
57. *Evening World-Herald*, "Slots in Use at City, County Private Clubs," August 24, 1949.
58. *Sunday World-Herald*, "Athletics Club's Slots Are Seized," September 25, 1949.
59. *Evening World-Herald*, "Athletic Club Faces Charges," September 27, 1949.
60. *Morning World-Herald*, "Trial January 15 for Athletic Club," December 30, 1950.
61. *Morning World-Herald*, "Allgaier Given Fine of $500," January 17, 1951.
62. *Evening World-Herald*, "Athletic Club Bought by 2," March 15, 1963.
63. *Omaha World-Herald*, "Athletic Club Closes Doors; Future Dim," September 4, 1970.
64. *Omaha World-Herald*, "Closing of Club Taken in Stride by Veteran Chef," September 5, 1970.
65. *Omaha World-Herald*, "Bank to Buy 2 Buildings," September 9, 1977; *Omaha World-Herald*, "In About Two Years Old Athletic Club Will Be Sold," October 24, 1983.
66. *Omaha World-Herald*, "Default Now Jeopardizes Office-Hotel Proposal; Public Auction Set for June 5 on Fed Block," April 27, 1989; *Omaha World-Herald*, "Athletic Club Blasted into Rubble," February 10, 1992.

Chapter 2

67. *Lincoln Journal Star*, "Omaha's Peony Park Was Once a Top Lincoln Highway Venue," January 2, 2005; *Evening World-Herald*, "Fighting Spirit Revealed in Jerry Malec's Death," November 23, 1937.
68. *Morning World-Herald*, "Peony Park Pavilion Destroyed by Flames," February 23, 1925; *Evening World-Herald*, "Peony Park," May 30, 1925.
69. *World-Herald*, "6.62 Inch Rainfall Floods a Vast Area," August 13, 1932; *Evening World-Herald*, "Loss Is $200,000 in Papio Flood," June 3, 1943; *Evening World-Herald*, "Flooding So Swift It Didn't Dampen Low Dance Floor," June 4, 1943; *Evening World-Herald*, "Peony Park Will Reopen Tomorrow," June 25, 1943.
70. *Sunday World-Herald*, "Peony News," March 30, 1958; *Omaha World-Herald*, "Peony Opens 'Wonderland,'" May 30, 1958.
71. *Sunday World-Herald*, "Rural Zoning Approved by City Planners," April 21, 1940; *Omaha World-Herald*, "Board Stands Firm on Annexing Peony," July 17, 1958; *Omaha World-Herald*, "Council Votes to Take Peony Park into City," July 23, 1958; *Lincoln Journal Star*, "Omaha's Peony Park Was Once a Top Lincoln Highway Venue," January 2, 2005.
72. *Evening World-Herald*, "Grand Opening," June 6, 1934.
73. *Omaha World-Herald*, "Sun-Up Interview: Joseph Malec, Sr.," October 21, 1967.
74. *Omaha World-Herald*, "The Party's Over; Dancers Say Goodbye," March 31, 1994.
75. *Omaha World-Herald*, "Peony Park Will Be Missed," June 18, 1996.
76. *Sunday World-Herald*, "Swimming Is the Most Healthful of All the Summer Sports," July 24, 1932.
77. *Evening World-Herald*, "Civil Rights Charge Filed," September 7, 1954; *Evening World-Herald*, "Peony Park Pays Rights' Case Fine," September 16, 1954.
78. *Omaha World-Herald*, "Civil Rights Charge Filed Against Peony," June 15, 1963; *Evening World-Herald*, "Urban League Says Complaint Is Rejected," July 5, 1963.
79. *Sunday World-Herald*, "Peony Turns Back Negros," July 14, 1963; *Omaha World-Herald*, "Peony Park Gates Reopen for Business," July 15, 1963.
80. *Evening World-Herald*, "Demonstrations Can Lead to No Good, Says Morrison," July 16, 1963.
81. *Evening World-Herald*, "Peony Park Locks Its Gates as Racial Pressure Increases," July 17, 1963; *Evening World-Herald*, "Peony Park Open as Club," July 18, 1963.

82. *Evening World-Herald*, "Negros Rap Peony Move," July 18, 1963; *Evening World-Herald*, "Mayor: Club Idea 'Solves,'" July 19, 1963.
83. *Evening World-Herald*, "'Both Races Are Refused,'" July 23, 1963; *Evening World-Herald*, "Park for All Peony's Hope," July 25, 1963.
84. *Omaha World-Herald*, "Military Bases May Place Segregated Places Off Limits," July 27, 1963; *Omaha World-Herald*, "Negros Use Peony's Pool," July 27, 1963; *Evening World-Herald*, "Negros Go to Peony Pool," July 29, 1963.
85. *Evening World-Herald*, "Peony Fined $25 in Suit by Negro," September 24, 1963; *Evening World-Herald*, "Peony's Fine Is $25 Again," September 30, 1963; *Evening World-Herald*, "McVoy: Magazine Didn't Get a True Picture of Negroes' Problems Here," December 3, 1963.
86. *Omaha World-Herald*, "When Peony Banned Blacks," February 13, 1994.
87. *Omaha World-Herald*, "City May Permit Roller Coasters," January 28, 1970; *Sunday World-Herald*, "Amusement Parks Follow Disney Lead," July 18, 1976; *Sunday World-Herald*, "Fun Close to Home," July 18, 1976; *Omaha World-Herald*, "Restraint Safety of Ride Disputed," August 5, 1978.
88. *Omaha World-Herald*, "Peony Park Files for Bankruptcy Protection—Court Action Won't Still Rides, Manager Pledges," March 24, 1992; *Omaha World-Herald*, "Saving Peony Impossible, Peschio Says Designating It a Landmark Called Futile," March 29, 1994; *Omaha World-Herald*, "Memories and Bids Fill the Air at Peony," April 17, 1994.
89. *Omaha World-Herald*, "Developer Says Plans in Works for Peony Site," March 24, 1994; *Omaha World-Herald*, "Group Joins Fight to Retain Peony as Park," January 5, 1995.
90. *Evening World-Herald*, "New Ak-Sar-Ben Site on West Center Street," March 24, 1919; *Evening World-Herald*, "Booming Ak-Sar-Ben Exposition Field," April 5, 1919; *Evening World-Herald*, "Begin Work on Track at Ak-Sar-Ben Field," May 27, 1919; *Sunday World-Herald*, "Ak-Sar-Ben Track Ready for Speed Monday," June 1, 1919.
91. *Morning World-Herald*, "Perfect Day for Opening Omaha's New Race Track," September 15, 1920; *Morning World-Herald*, "Big Grandstand Packed Full on Ak-Sar-Ben Field," September 17, 1920. News of the races shared the headlines that day with reports of a bombing on Wall Street that killed 38 and injured 143.
92. Leslie Valentine, "The Development of the Omaha Municipal Airfield, 1924–1930," *Nebraska History* 61 (1980): 401.
93. For a more detailed discussion of the transcontinental airmail flight in 1921, see Henry Ladd Smith, *Airways: The History of Commercial Aviation in the United States* (Washington, D.C.: Smithsonian Institution Press, 1991),

67–71, and William Leary, *Aerial Pioneers: The U.S. Air Mail Service, 1918–1927* (Washington, D.C.: Smithsonian Institution Press, 1985), 140–44.

94. Valentine, "Omaha Municipal Airfield," 402.

95. *World-Herald*, "First Ak-Sar-Ben Call Brings 232 Responses," January 17, 1928; *Morning World-Herald*, "AK's Coliseum Contract Is Let; To Start at Once," March 15, 1928; *Evening World-Herald*, "Ak-Sar-Ben to Spend Additional $175,000," April 9, 1928; *Evening World-Herald*, "Ak-Sar-Ben Launches 5,000 Members Drive," May 19, 1928; *Morning World-Herald*, "Lay Cornerstone of AK Coliseum at Field Today," May 25, 1928; *Morning World-Herald*, "Ak-Sar-Ben Membership Is Increased to 4,739," May 26, 1928.

96. *Evening World-Herald*, "Coronation Ball Most Important Event on Today's Social Calendar," October 12, 1928; *Morning World-Herald*, "Emma Nash Is Ak-Sar-Ben Queen," October 13, 1928.

97. *Evening World-Herald*, "Ak-Sar-Ben's Horse Show on Tonight," November 5, 1928; *Sunday World-Herald*, "Races Made Most Money Last Year," December 30, 1928.

98. *Sunday World-Herald*, "Skaters and Thoroughbred Horses…Step Out and Jump…At Ak-Sar-Ben Show Next Sunday," October 16, 1938; *Evening World-Herald*, "Hockey Plant Is Assured for Coliseum," September 12, 1939; *Morning World-Herald*, "Start Work on Ice Today," October 2, 1939; *Sunday World-Herald*, "Plan Special Ceremony at Hockey Inaugural," November 12, 1939.

99. *Sunday World-Herald*, "Omahans Form Skating Clubs for Use of Coliseum Rink," November 12, 1939.

100. Omaha—1935 Triple Crown Winner, www.triplecrownraces.com/omaha (accessed July 29, 2016).

101. *Evening World-Herald*, "Ak Track Has New Surface," January 3, 1966.

102. *Evening World-Herald*, "They Came, They Saw…," April 1, 1966; *Sunday World-Herald*, "1,400 to Eat at New Hall," April 17, 1966; *Evening World-Herald*, "Ak-Sar-Ben Dedicates a New Hall, Coliseum," April 21, 1966; *Sunday World-Herald*, "Ak-Sar-Ben Renovation Is 'Like Magic,'" May 1, 1966; *Sunday World-Herald*, "New Banquet Hall Seats 18 Hundred in Regal Fashion," May 1, 1966.

103. *Omaha World-Herald*, "Will Other Shoe Drop?," February 4, 1996.

104. *Omaha World-Herald*, "For Council Bluffs Greyhound Races, It's the Finish Line," December 21, 2015.

105. *Omaha World-Herald*, "County Officially Buys Ak-Sar-Ben," April 30, 1992; *Omaha World-Herald*, "Ak's 1991 Loss of $2 Million Is Second Largest," June 14, 1992.

106. *Omaha World-Herald*, "Talks Fail on Loan to Save AK Racing—RaceCo Votes Not to Hold Live '96 Meet," February 16, 1996; *Omaha World-Herald*, "Keeping Rest of Ak Open Next Struggle—Nonracing Side Has Shortfall in Funding," February 17, 1996.
107. *Omaha World-Herald*, "How Did Ak-Sar-Ben Come to This?" February 18, 1996.
108. *Omaha World-Herald*, "What to Do With AK? Ideas Flow—Architects Hear of Arena, Dorms," February 29, 1996.
109. *Omaha World-Herald*, "$40 Million First Data Plan Links Its Offices Ak, UNO," May 20, 1996; *Omaha World-Herald*, "Group Presents Ak Plan for FDR-UNO Joint Use," June 18, 1996; *Omaha World-Herald*, "5–1 Decision Advances FDR Plan, Mrs. Borgeson Votes 'No,' Backs Racing," July 16, 1996; *Omaha World-Herald*, "Vote Puts FDR Plan in Motion—Ak Land Sale OK'd; Work Could Begin in May," January 1, 1997.
110. *Omaha World-Herald*, "Omaha's Love Affair on Ice, City Has Embraced Hockey for More Than 50 Years," October 12, 1997.
111. *Omaha World-Herald*, "Board: AK Coliseum on Last Legs," August 24, 1999; *Omaha World-Herald*, "Closing the Barn Doors: An Ice Age Ends for Omaha's Hockey Tradition," March 20, 2002; *Omaha World-Herald*, "Will Rest of Ak Land Be Academic Turf?," December 18, 2002.
112. *Omaha World-Herald*, "Ak Vision: Be a Destination Again," May 24, 2005; *Omaha World-Herald*, "AK-SAR-BEN Site History," September 30, 2006; *Omaha World-Herald*, "Village to Rise Where Horses Raced," October 27, 2007.

Chapter 3

113. Jack Kerouac, *On the Road* (New York: Penguin Books, 2011), 16.
114. Jobbers Canyon Historic District, National Register of Historic Places Inventory—Nomination Form, United States Department of the Interior, National Park Service.
115. *Omaha World-Herald*, "What's There," October 7, 1987.
116. Ibid.
117. Daly Bednarek, "Creating an 'Image Center,'" 194–96; *New York Times*, "Historic District at Issue in Omaha," December 13, 1997; *Omaha World-Herald*, "Judge Rules for City on Canyon," May 17, 1988; *Omaha World-Herald*, "Demolition Continues, Round Two Complete in Jobbers Canyon Suit," December 15, 1988; *Omaha World-Herald*, "Judge Refuses to Halt

Jobbers Canyon Work," February 15, 1989; *Omaha World-Herald*, "Court Out of Way: Jobbers Clear in 45 Days," June 13, 1989.

118. *Omaha World-Herald*, "Companies Get More Space, Jobbers Canyon Moves Seen as Improvements," July 5, 1988.

119. *Omaha World-Herald*, "Sonja Henie's Heart Was Lost in Omaha," February 10, 2003.

120. *Omaha World-Herald*, "ConAgra's Next Home a Sore Point for Omaha," October 4, 2015.

121. *Omaha World-Herald*, "The McKesson & Robbins Building, Industrial Structure Serves as Municipal Memento," September 10, 1986; *Omaha World-Herald*, "Pendleton of Nebraska Quietly Gains in Stature," July 26, 1981.

122. *Omaha World-Herald*, "Omahans Weigh Cost of Destroying Jobbers Canyon to Make Way for ConAgra Campus," October 1, 2015.

123. *Omaha World-Herald*, "Building History," February 25, 1990; Sorenson, *Story of Omaha*, 224–28.

124. *Evening World-Herald*, "Farewell Services at St. Philomena's," October 14, 1907; *Omaha World-Herald*, "Change Comes to Omaha City," March 13, 1988.

125. Sorenson, *Story of Omaha*, 602–11.

126. *Sunday World-Herald*, "One Time Giant of City Packing Says Goodbye," April 23, 1967.

127. *Omaha World-Herald*, "Armour Crew Accepts Close, but Only Sadly," June 28, 1968; *Sunday World-Herald*, "Armour Closing to Slow Meat Production," June 23, 1968.

128. *Omaha World-Herald*, "Omaha Swift Plant 'Too Old for Profit,'" October 31, 1968.

129. *Omaha World-Herald*, "Wilson Packing Plant Closing Doors Today," April 2, 1976.

130. *Omaha World-Herald*, "Armour Crew Accepts Close, but Only Sadly," June 28, 1968; *Sunday World-Herald*, "Armour Closing to Slow Meat Production," June 23, 1968.

131. *Omaha World-Herald*, "Closing Is Sad at Swift Plant," July 3, 1969.

132. *Omaha World-Herald*, "Armour Crew Accepts Close, but Only Sadly," June 28, 1968.

133. *Omaha World-Herald*, "New Muscle Bulges after Lean Decade," April 23, 1976; *Omaha World-Herald*, "Metro Tech to Become a Catalyst," April 23, 1976.

134. *Omaha World-Herald*, "Wrecking Ball Chases Glebe Out," April 10, 1999; *Omaha World-Herald*, "Blam! Blam! From Building to Dust in 18

Seconds," November 2, 2002; *Omaha World-Herald*, "Building Fulfills Dream," November 6, 2009.

135. *Omaha World-Herald*, "Taking Stock, May South Omahans Greet Proposed Redevelopment with Cautious Optimism," December 19, 1997.

136. *Omaha World-Herald*, "Memories Replace Livestock on Auction Block," August 22, 1999; *Omaha World-Herald*, "Final Sale Closes Curtain on Stockyards' Grand Era," October 27, 1999; *Omaha World-Herald*, "For the Stockyards, This Sale Was Final," October 28, 1999.

137. Livestock Exchange Building, National Register of Historic Places Registration Form, United States Department of the Interior, National Park Service, May 29, 1999.

138. *New York Times*, "Historic District at Issue in Omaha," December 13, 1987.

Chapter 4

139. Judy Horan, "Back to the River," Omaha Magazine.Com, omahamagazine.com/tag/american-smelting-and-refining-co (retrieved December 13, 2016).

140. Sorenson, *Story of Omaha*, 579–81.

141. *Morning World-Herald*, "Finest Plant in Land, Daniel Guggenheim of Executive Board of American Smelting Co. Inspects Omaha Refinery," October 21, 1901.

142. *Omaha World-Herald*, "World's Largest Lead Refinery Is in Omaha," April 30, 1925.

143. *Omaha World-Herald*, October 27, 1929.

144. *Sunday World-Herald*, "Biggest Lead Refinery," April 3, 1949.

145. Ibid.

146. Omaha Planning Department, "Omaha Master Plan Report No. 264 (revised): Concept Element" (City of Omaha, September 1995), 2. 7.

147. *Omaha World-Herald*, "U.P. Selects Site Downtown, the Rail Giant Will Build Its New Headquarters across the Street from Its Present Location," November 1, 2000; *Omaha World-Herald*, "U.P. Opens Up, New Office Headquarters Adds to City's Increasing Shine," June 6, 2004.

148. *Omaha World-Herald*, "Omaha Skyline Climbs, First National Bank to Build 40 Stories of Glass, Granite, First National Bank Center Coming Thursday," September 23, 1998.

149. *Omaha World-Herald*, "Office Park to Reshape Downtown, Bank, Omaha World-Herald Plan Major Projects, Downtown Projects," October 23, 1996.
150. *Omaha World-Herald*, "ASARCO Has Omaha Plans, $6.7 Million on Tap for Improvements," March 22, 1989; *Omaha World-Herald*, "Lead Level in Air Rises Downtown; EPA Says Lower It, Clean Air Act's Passage to Bring Nebraska Money," June 29, 1990.
151. *Omaha World-Herald*, "Asarco Expects to Close Unless Deadline Eased," May 22, 1993; *Omaha World-Herald*, "Refinery Plans Strategy to Cut Lead Emissions, Parks Director Says Riverfront Will Be Safer, ASARCO Lead Output," June 17, 1993; *Omaha World-Herald*, "State Says Refinery on Track, ASARCO Cleanup Discussed at Hearing," December 16, 1993.
152. *Omaha World-Herald*, "Suit Filed Against Asarco; Company Sues State Agency," March 15, 1994; *Omaha World-Herald*, "EPA Files Suit to Prevent Discharges from Asarco," April 5, 1994.
153. *Omaha World-Herald*, "Riverfront Plan Would Move Asarco, Riverfront Businesses," March 8, 1995; *Omaha World-Herald*, "Park Viewed as Jewel in Plans for Riverfront, Riverfront Businesses," March 9, 1995; *Omaha World-Herald*, "Park Supporter Says Plans Could Mesh," March 10, 1995.
154. For a sense of the course of the lawsuits, the various negotiations and the final deals see *Omaha World-Herald*, "Asarco, Government Propose Agreement, Deal Would Impose Fines, Settle Claims Asarco Case," June 29, 1995; *Omaha World-Herald*, "Suit Settled, Asarco Looks at Relocation," January 9, 1996; *Omaha World-Herald*, "City, Asarco Reach Agreement on Site, Firm to Vacate Refinery; Area to Be Park," April 13, 1996; *Omaha World-Herald*, "Asarco Agreement Clears the Way," April 18, 1996; *Omaha World-Herald*, "Council Gets Behind Asarco Cleanup Plan, Amendment Born of Concern Over City's Liability," July 31, 1996; *Omaha World-Herald*, "Asarco Accelerates Plan, Will Close July 1," February 15, 1997; *Omaha World-Herald*, "Asarco Cleanup Plan Wins State Approval; The Ruling Requires that the Property be Turned Over to the City or a 'City-Created Entity' after the Site Is Cleaned," September 5, 1997; *Omaha World-Herald*, "The Asarco Plan Opens Door to Better Times on Riverfront," June 4, 1998; *Omaha World-Herald*, "City, Asarco Sign Deal to Turn Plant to Park; Asarco Park Plan; Asarco Liability Amendment," June 10, 1998; *Omaha World-Herald*, "Asarco, Omaha Negotiators Did Well," June 10, 1998; *Omaha World-Herald*, "Asarco Hires Firm to Demolish Refinery Site," August 13, 1998.

155. *Omaha World-Herald*, "Asarco Site to Become Park by 1999, Plant Closing Means Loss of 225 Jobs, Asarco History," April 15, 1996.
156. *Omaha World-Herald*, "Lead Plan Carries Big Price Tag," December 29, 2001; *Omaha World-Herald*, "The Racial Litmus Test," January 23, 2002; *Omaha World-Herald*, "Research to Analyze Lead Level in Omaha," February 2, 2003; *Omaha World-Herald*, "Omaha Nears Superfund Era," April 30, 2003; "EPA Superfund Program, Omaha Lead, Omaha NE," cumulis.epa.gov/supercpad/cursites/csitinfo.cfm?id=0703481 (accessed December 23, 2016).

Conclusion

157. *Evening World-Herald*, "Old Bridge Was a 'Bride' in 1888," November 21, 1966.
158. *Evening World-Herald*, "'Dream of Decades' Bridge Events Near," September 24, 1947.
159. *Omaha World-Herald*, "Span Carries 'Last' Vehicle," November 21, 1966; *Omaha World-Herald*, "Bridge Near Close Again," December 12, 1966.
160. *Omaha World-Herald*, "Cities Ask States' Aid for Bridge," November 29, 1966; *Omaha World-Herald*, "AkBridge Fate Is Tossed Back into State's Lap," May 23, 1967.
161. *Sunday World-Herald*, "Demolition Helping to Build an Architectural Education," December 15, 1968.

INDEX

P

R

S

T

U

V

W

ABOUT THE AUTHOR

Janet R. Daly Bednarek was born and raised in Omaha, Nebraska. She grew up in the Cathedral (now called Midtown) neighborhood, attending St. Cecilia's Grade School and Cathedral High School. With a major in history, she graduated from Creighton University and then went to the University of Pittsburgh for her PhD. After a brief stint as a public historian working for the United States Air Force, she joined the faculty at the University of Dayton in 1992. Her classes include American Urban History, History of American City Planning and History of American Aviation. She has published four books, including her first, based on her dissertation, *The Changing Image of the City: Planning for Downtown Omaha, 1945–1973*. Her latest book, *Airports, Cities and the Jet Age*, came out in 2016. She lives with her husband in Centerville, Ohio.